THE PENNSYLVANIA LEGISLATIVE REAPPORTIONMENT OF 1991

Ken Gormley, Executive Director, Legislative Reapportionment Commission
Associate Professor, Duquesne University School of Law

© Copyright 1994
Pennsylvania Legislative Reapportionment Commission

ISBN 0-8182-0191-6

Commonwealth of Pennsylvania, Bureau of Publications

This book is dedicated to Barbara Butterfield Janecko, Executive Secretary of the Legislative Reapportionment Commission, who performed endless hours of uncompensated work — over a period of three years — to ensure the success of each aspect of the reapportionment project including this publication. Her work exemplified the spirit of the true citizen-public servant, who works for the sake of work; seeks perfection for the sake of perfection; and asks no reward but to benefit the collectivity known as the Commonwealth.

Additional thanks to: John Shaw, Esquire; Kathy Jeffrey, and the Department of General Services, Bureau of Publications, Design and Typesetting Unit; LuAnn Driscoll, Karen Knochel, Darlene Mocello, Carolyn Rohan, Barbara Salopek, of the Word Processing Center at the University of Pittsburgh School of Law; and Leslie Kozler, all of whom performed invaluable work in preparing this manuscript for publication.

Finally, this publication could not have been completed without the hard work and dedication of Eric Meyer, of the Bureau of Publications, who passed away (too young), shortly before the manuscript was completed. This book, that will serve to educate citizens for generations, stands as a tribute to his memory.

FOREWORD

By Patricia DeCarlo
Co-Chair, Philadelphia Latino
Voting Rights Committee
Philadelphia, PA

As our society inches towards the 21st century and the population of the United States continues to transform itself dramatically — in color of skin, income level, and cultural-ethnic background — there must of necessity be changes in the existing power structure in government, to honestly reflect these changes.

The genius of "redistricting" our legislature each decade, a process built into our Constitution, is that it provides an institutional tool by which to prevent those in power from unjustly clinging to it. Human nature dictates that those holding political power and wealth will have little incentive to surrender it. Yet reapportionment, and the constitutional precept of one-person-one-vote, arm the average citizen with the ability — indeed the obligation — to stand guard over the fair distribution of power and resources for all people, and thus make a democracy that is true and vibrant.

By the arrival of the 21st century, citizens of various colors and ethnic origins — Latinos, African-Americans and Asian Americans — will comprise a piece of the "majority" in this country. The only viable tool that ethnic minorities will possess to ensure a proportionate right to vote, and to elect representatives of their own choice in Harrisburg and Washington, is the constitutionally-mandated tool of redistricting. This, along with the Federal Voting Rights Act, embodies the simple guaranty of our democracy dating back to the Revolutionary War — that there will exist no permanent aristocracy; that the fortunes and opportunities of all citizens will remain fluid and able to rise through hard work.

In this sense, the lessons of past reapportionments are "required knowledge" for all minority citizens in this Commonwealth. They are essential for all citizens, of whatever heritage. One must understand how reapportionment works in order to prod the machinery of government and make it function for the better.

During the past several reapportionments in Pennsylvania, the Latino and African-American communities have had a noticeable, positive impact. The Reapportionment Commission has encouraged citizens in a very positive way to attend hearings, provide testimony, and put their views on the table. Although not all views have led to new district lines on a map, these views have been expressed, and heard. Many of them have been acted upon.

Reapportionment is a wondrous invention. It allows all citizens of all backgrounds and colors to air their views; influence the balance of power; and eventually become part of the balance of power in government. But to use reapportionment skillfully, like any tool, one must contribute attention to detail and hard work.

The following book on the Pennsylvania Legislative Reapportionment of 1991 provides a starting point for that important endeavor. The rest is left to the individual citizen, who must bring the guarantees of our Constitution to life with diligence and active participation in a healthy process that sparks democracy to life once each decade. Reapportionment of legislative seats is an easy enough process. Citizen participation in that process is what makes it difficult, but invaluable if our constitutional republic is to survive.

PREFACIO

Por: Patricia DeCarlo
Co-Presidenta del Comite Lantino de Philadelphia
para la Redistribucion Electoral
Philadelphia, PA

Mientras nuestra sociedad se aproxima al siglo XXI y la poblacion de los Estados Unidos continua una transformacion drastica — en el color de la piel, nivel de ingreso, y decendencia cultural y etnica, tiene que haber, por necesidad, cambios en la estructura de poder que existe en el gobierno, para que honestamente se reflejen estos cambios.

El genio de "realinear nuestros Distritos Legislativos" cada decada, un proceso integrado en nuestra Constitucion, es que provee un instrumento institucional con el cual se puede impedir que aquellos con poder injustamente se adhieran a el. La naturaleza humana dicta que aquellos que tienen poder politico y riqueza tendran poco incentivo para ceder su poder. Sin embargo, realineacion de distritos electorales y el principio constitucional de una-persona un voto, arma al ciudadano ordinario con la abilidad — y obligacion — de montar guardia para asegurar una distribucion justa de poder y recursos para toda la gente, y para lograr una democracia que es verdadera y vibrante.

Para la llegada del siglo XXI, cuidadanos de varios colores y origen etnico — Latinos, Africano-Americanos y Asiatico-Americanos — pasaran a ser parte de la "majoria" en este pais. El unico instrumento viable que la minoria etnica tendra para asegurar que ellos tendran un derecho al voto proporcional, y elegir representes de su preferencia en Harrisburg y Washington, es el instrumento constitucional de realineacion de distrito electoral. Esto, en compañia con el Acta Federal de Derecho al Voto, encarna la simple garantia de que en nuestra democracia, desde la Guerra Revolucionaria — no existira una aristrocracia permanente; que las fortunas y las oportuniadades de todos los cuidadanos permaneceran fluente y capaz de progresar por medio de trabajo fuerte.

En el mismo sentido, las lecciones aprendidas en realineaciones pasadas son "conocimientos requeridos" y esenciales para todo cuidadano minoritario o de origen etnico en este estado. Uno tiene que entender como trabaja la realineacion para poder influenciar la maquinaria del gobierno y hacer que funcione mejor.

Durante las ultimas redistribuciones de districtos electorales en Pennsylvania, las comunidades Latinas, y Africanas-Americanas han tenido un impacto notable y positivo. La Comision Para Redistribucion Electoral anima a los ciudadanos en una manera positiva que asistan a vistas publicas, provean testimonio, y pongan sus puntos de vistas en la mesa. Aunque no todo los testimonios han traido nuevas lineas a los distritos electorales en los mapas, estos puntos de vistas han sido expresados, escuchados y muchos han sido usado como referencia en los cambios.

Redistribucion electoral es un invento maravilloso. Le permite a todo cuidadano de toda clase de descendencia y color a exponer sus puntos de vistas; influenciar el balance de poder; y finalmente ser parte de este poder en el gobierno. Pero para usar redistribucion electoral sabiamente, como cualquier otro instrumento, uno tiene que ponerle atencion al detalle y trabajo fuerte.

El siguiente libro de la Redistribucion Legislativa del estado de Pennsylvania de 1991 provee un punto de comienzo para ese esfuerzo importante. Lo demas se le deja al cuidadano individual, quien tiene que traer la garantia de nuestra Constitucion a la vida con deligencia y participacion activa en un proceso saludable que brinda una chispa de vida a la democracia una vez cada decada. El proceso de Redistribucion. Legislativa es facil. La participacion de cuidadanos en este proceso es lo que lo hace dificil, pero de gran valor, si la Constitucion de nuestra Republica ha de sobrevivir.

TABLE OF CONTENTS

I.
INTRODUCTION

Each decade following the federal census, the Constitution of Pennsylvania requires that the legislative districts for the House and Senate of Pennsylvania be newly drawn, or reapportioned. The Pennsylvania Constitution mandates this process so that each citizen's vote ultimately carries the same weight in the ballot box. Equality in voting is meant to remain constant regardless of a population shifting from rural, to urban, to suburban areas, or the changing racial compositions in neighborhoods and political subdivisions.

The Legislative Reapportionment of 1991, by almost any historical yardstick, turned into one of the most colorful and challenging redistricting enterprises since the Pennsylvania Constitution of 1776 first introduced the concept of periodic legislative reapportionment to the United States. In 1991, the problems of creating legislative districts that satisfied the U.S. Supreme Court's one-person-one-vote mandate — problems that had dominated the reapportionment process since the U.S. Supreme Court handed down its landmark 1962 decision in *Baker v. Carr* — took a backseat to other issues. For the first time, modern computer software enabled legislative staffs to effortlessly generate maps with extremely low population deviations. Legislative seats containing roughly equivalent percentages of raw population could be created in infinitely different ways, with a ream of different color-coded maps.

The bigger question, however, was "how" to create such equal-sized configurations. Should staffers at sterile computer terminals be permitted to ignore communities of interest and disrupt traditional political equations in the name of fashioning legislative districts with lower and lower population deviations? Prior reapportionments that had created maps in smoke-filled rooms with only pen and paper had at least managed to place a premium on old-fashioned political fairness. Modern technological wizardry now threatened to create mischief. The Reapportionment Commission's single greatest challenge in 1991 was not to create equal-sized districts; rather, its more difficult task was to create districts even-handedly.

A second challenge related to the guaranty of equality in the right to vote for all citizens, embodied in the Fifteenth Amendment of the United States Constitution. A bold new development in the interpretation of the Federal Voting Rights Act, by Congress and the United States Supreme Court, thrust upon the Commission an unparalleled mandate to create districts that not only protected, but affirmatively assisted, African-American, Latino, Asian-American, and other minority groups in electing candidates of choice. Computers could produce these "racially gerrymandered" districts, but should they try?

Finally, the shifting population of the 1980s — from the urban western part of Pennsylvania to the suburban east — created a third surprise (and no-win situation) for the Commission. One senator and a handful of representatives would eventually lose their seats in the tumultuous reapportionment process. The central focus of this uproar would turn out to be Senator Frank Pecora (R, 44th District), whose Allegheny County seat would be moved east due to population shifts; he would wage appeals unsuccessfully up to the United States Supreme Court; he would re-claim his seat as a transplanted resident of Montgomery County; and he would then switch his registration to "Democrat," triggering a political free-for-all in the Senate chambers in Harrisburg and a federal lawsuit by voters in eastern Pennsylvania. How would the Commission deal with this unexpected political nightmare? Would the Reapportionment Plan survive the multi-faceted legal challenges intact?

The Legislative Reapportionment Commission, created by Article II, Section 17 of the Pennsylvania Constitution, has been a unique hybrid body since it was first conceived. It allows four legislators and a single apolitical chairman to exercise power akin to the State Legislature itself. The Pennsylvania Constitution delegates vast authority to such a small contingency; the legislature and judiciary have few opportunities to undo a redistricting map once it is lawfully promulgated by the Commission.[1]

The distinguishing feature of this curious body, as established by the state constitution in 1968, is that (at least in theory) it mixes political and apolitical forces to yield a measure of neutrality in an otherwise rough-and-tumble world of politics. This is accomplished by mixing four highly-politicized members with one neutral swing-vote. In 1991, under the terms of Article II, Section 17 of the Constitution, the Commission consisted of the Majority Leader of the Senate (Republican Senator F. Joseph Loeper), the Minority Leader of the Senate (Democratic Senator Robert J. Mellow), the Majority Leader of the House (Democratic Representative H. William DeWeese, who deputized Representative Allen G. Kukovich), and the Minority Leader of the House (Republican Representative Matthew J. Ryan, who deputized Representative John M. Perzel). The Constitution provided that these four members of the Commission would select the fifth member, to serve as Chairman.

In 1991, however, the four legislative members failed to agree on a candidate for Chairman. The matter was thrown to the Pennsylvania Supreme Court, as provided by Article II, Section 17. The Court promptly appointed Robert J. Cindrich, a well-respected Pittsburgh attorney and a former U.S. Attorney for the Western District of Pennsylvania, known for his tenacity, sense of fairness, and appreciation for constitutional principles.

Chairman Cindrich ultimately forged a plan that represented a unique step forward for Pennsylvania. The reapportionment plan which eventually received the Commission's stamp of approval — through a divided, yet bi-partisan vote — placed a substantially greater emphasis on minority voting rights than any previous reapportionment plan in Pennsylvania history. The plan was solid enough to survive over twenty-five challenges in the Pennsylvania Supreme Court and a handful of suits in federal court.

As this publication will illustrate, the success of the 1991 Reapportionment Plan was largely accomplished as a result of the tireless efforts, input, and criticism offered by citizens and groups throughout Pennsylvania. The inherently political process of redistricting legislative seats remains imperfect — even two centuries after Pennsylvania introduced the egalitarian notion of reapportionment to the nation. At the same time, technology and enhanced citizen participation have opened the door to vast improvements from the days of smoke-filled rooms and hand-drawn maps guided only by concerns for incumbency and political advantage.

The challenge facing legislators, citizens, and Commission members alike in the year 2001, and for generations into the future, will be the bridling of technology and the harnessing of a growing archive of information from reapportionment ex-

---

[1]   The process followed by the Legislative Reapportionment Commission is thus quite distinct from the process followed in reapportioning United States congressional seats in Pennsylvania. The latter task is left to the Pennsylvania Legislature as a body.

periences of the past. Even before the reapportionment of 1991, Pennsylvania had made significant strides since those days pre-dating *Baker v. Carr* and *Reynolds v. Sims*, when reapportionment was sporadic and equality in districts lay in the jaded eyes of the beholder. As a historic matter, Pennsylvania may have been ahead of its time in creating a strong base of minority representation and leadership in the House and Senate, even before the Federal Voting Rights Act of 1965 mandated the creation of minority districts. Yet solidification of such advances will not come easily. Only vigorous citizen participation and self-imposed legislative restraint will ensure that future reapportionment maps continue to embody the marked progress which reflects the evolution of a civilized, democratic republic.

This publication is prepared for the purpose of preserving an otherwise evanescent history of the Legislative Reapportionment Commission experience of 1991 — an experience which spanned three years and dozens of lawsuits. It is dedicated to a simple proposition: that those who govern, and those who are governed alike, are capable of improving upon history's trials and errors — but only through education and enlightened diligence.

II.
HISTORY OF REAPPORTIONMENT IN PENNSYLVANIA

A. Early History

In early colonial Pennsylvania, legislative districts in the modern sense were nonexistent. William Penn's second *Frame of Government* in 1683 established the county as the basic unit of representation and populated the legislature with a fixed number of representatives from each county.[2] Penn's *Frame of Government* provided that the number of legislative representatives should be increased from time to time based upon "the increase and multiplying of the people."[3] Despite this vague attempt at regrouping, Penn's *Frame of Government* contained no mechanism to adjust the number of representatives as populations began to vary from county to county.

The Quakers, predominantly living in southeastern Pennsylvania, sought to use this county-based system of representation to maintain control of the General Assembly. While initially balanced, Penn's apportionment scheme became increasingly inequitable as the eastern cities, particularly Philadelphia, expanded rapidly and as new counties sprang up in the western portion of Pennsylvania. For example, by 1752, the General Assembly was composed of thirty-six members. Twenty-six of these came from the well-entrenched counties of Chester, Bucks, and Philadelphia (only two came from the city of Philadelphia itself). In contrast, the western "back-counties" inhabited by poor Scotch-Irish settlers could claim only ten representatives, despite the fact that their population of tax-paying citizens (i.e. voters) exceeded that of the Easterners.[4] In other words, those in power kept their power by maintaining the *status quo* regarding the apportionment of legislators.

During the midst of the Revolutionary War, with the adoption of the first Pennsylvania Constitution in September of 1776 and the inevitable decrease in power of the Quakers (due to their pacifist convictions), the skewed balance of representation in the General Assembly was finally addressed. As a first step, the General Assembly in March of 1776 added seventeen new representatives from the western counties and Philadelphia City,[5] recognizing the growing presence of these regions. Second, to preserve a more even-handed system of apportionment, Section 17 of the new Constitution explicitly recognized that "representation in proportion to the number of taxable inhabitants is the only principle that can at all times secure liberty and make the voice of a majority of the people the law of the land ..."[6]

The old practice of providing a fixed number of representatives for each county, regardless of population, would continue for only two years. Lists of taxable inhabitants within the Commonwealth were prepared.[7] Thereafter, the General Assembly identified taxable citizens in each county and Philadelphia, and "ap-

---

[2]   JANELLE HOBBS, REAPPORTIONMENT IN PENNSYLVANIA: A HISTORY OF THE RE-APPORTIONMENT PROCESS AND THE LEGISLATIVE REAPPORTIONMENT COMMIS-SION 3 (1981).

[3]   *Id.*

[4]   *Id.* at 4.

[5]   *Id.* at 6.

[6]   PA. CONST. of 1776, §17.

[7]   *Id.* Temporarily, six representatives were assigned to the city of Philadelphia and six to each county. The term of office was one year.

point[ed] a representative to each, in proportion to the taxables in such returns ...."[8] Every seven years, the General Assembly prepared new tallies of the taxable inhabitants for each city and county and adjusted the number of representatives.[9] In other words, Pennsylvania established a scheme for reapportioning its legislature[10] as part of a broader effort to enfranchise its citizen/electors.

Subsequent overhauls of the Pennsylvania Constitution preserved the reapportionment provisions, although with constant tinkering and fine-tuning. The Constitution of 1790 switched from the ill-fated unicameral legislature to a bicameral body composed of a House and Senate, with the number of representatives set at no more than one hundred and no less than sixty.[11] The Constitution of 1790 also made both houses of the legislature subject to septennial reapportionment. Significantly, in establishing the new ground rules for redistricting, the 1790 Constitution provided that "[n]either the city of Philadelphia nor any county shall be divided in forming a district."[12] Thus, the integrity of city and county political boundaries was meant to be preserved.

The Constitution of 1838 generally maintained the *status quo* when it came to reapportionment, while making minor alterations in the election of senators.[13] It added a degree of flexibility by providing that *single*-member districts could not spill over city or county boundaries, while cities or counties entitled to *more* than two senators based upon population could now be subdivided into smaller districts (this included the city of Philadelphia).[14] Wards within Philadelphia were preserved against splits, in deference to the local politics of that city.[15] However, for the first time in the history of Pennsylvania, the Constitution of 1838 allowed traditional political boundaries to be disturbed, at least outside Philadelphia. The purpose, of course, was to move towards districts roughly equivalent in population.

The Constitution of 1873 yielded even more dramatic changes, primarily because of the heated debate during the Constitutional Convention of 1872-1873. This debate centered upon widespread corruption in the House and Senate after the Civil War, as Pennsylvania became more industrialized. Increasing the size of the legislature, it was argued, would help flush out this corruption. Altering the mode of the election would also help. The size of the House was thus increased from one hundred to two hundred. The size of the Senate was set at fifty. The Constitution now required the legislature to divide the state into districts based upon this ratio; thus, modern reapportionment was born.[16] The significant feature of this new redistricting scheme was that it was based upon *total population* rather

---

[8] *Id.*

[9] *Id.*

[10] *See A History of Pennsylvania Constitutions, in* 3 PENNSYLVANIA CONSTITUTIONAL CONVENTION — 1967-1968, at 2 [hereinafter *History of Pennsylvania Constitutions*].

[11] PA. CONST. of 1790, art. I, §4. Each county already in existence was guaranteed at least one representative. The number of senators was to be fixed by the legislature, and could not be less than one-fourth, nor greater than one-third the number of representatives. *Id.* §6. Each senatorial district, including the city of Philadelphia, could elect no more than four senators, based upon taxable inhabitants. *Id.* §7.

[12] *Id.* §7.

[13] The number of senators each district could elect was reduced from four to two. PA. CONST. of 1838, art. I, §7. At the same time, a city or county with sufficient population to elect more than two senators could be divided into districts and elect up to four senators within the political unit.

[14] *Id.* §7.

[15] *Id.*

[16] PA. CONST. of 1873, art. II, §§16-17.

than taxable population — each citizen was counted equally, regardless of property ownership. Districts were based strictly upon population; traditional political boundaries (i.e. city, county and other lines) would not govern.[17] The Constitution of 1873 also extended the period of reapportionment to ten years and selected the United States decennial census to serve as the yardstick of pure population.[18]

Although this new "ratio" method of reapportionment led to far greater equality among voters in the Commonwealth, disparities still existed. If one viewed the 1870 census figures, one observed that Allegheny County (as of 1874) had one senator per 87,400 people. Montgomery County had one senator for every 81,000. Fayette and Greene Counties had one senator for 69,000. However, the city of Philadelphia in 1874 had one senator for every 168,000 — a gross underrepresentation.[19]

Interestingly, the debates during the Constitutional Convention of 1873 included a fiery battle over whether a reapportionment commission should be created. Charles Buckalew, the Convention's Democratic leader, was a scholar of the Pennsylvania Constitution and the author of a book advocating proportional representation.[20] Buckalew criticized the (ultimately victorious) plan to have reapportionment conducted by the General Assembly itself, leery of incumbent gerrymandering to the detriment of citizens' voting rights. In Buckalew's mind, members of the House and Senate were propelled by "the seductive, silent, efficient action of self-interest."[21] Buckalew proposed the creation of a 12-member commission elected by the House and Senate to steer reapportionment. This proposal was roundly defeated.[22]

Representative Wayne McVeagh, the 1873 Convention's Republican leader, was more comfortable with the idea of the newly "reformed" legislature controlling the reapportionment process. He proposed that the Convention should set forth specific guidelines to limit legislative discretion, suggesting, for example, a requirement that no district reflect a deviation from the population norm of more than ten percent.[23] This proposal slipped through the cracks of the Convention's agenda, however, and reapportionment by the legislature was adopted as part of the Constitution of 1873 without any specific safeguards guiding the hand of the legislature in its map-making.

Because the Constitutional Convention of 1873 had failed to impose any strict requirements regarding the degree of population equality, compactness, or contiguity of territory required in formulating election districts, the 1874 legislature was able to engage in blatant political gerrymandering in sketching districts under the

---

[17] The only notable exception was that no county or city could possess more than one-sixth of the total number of senators, thus keeping a cap on Philadelphia's potential representation. *Id.* §16. In the House districts, cities and counties were not to be split (unless they contained population enough for more than one district), and each city or county split was required to be divided into districts "of compact and contiguous territory." *Id.* §17.

[18] *Id.* §18.

[19] HOBBS, *supra* note 2, at 8-9. This was in large part due to the cap imposed on cities and counties built into art. II, §16.

[20] *Id.* at 10 & n.11.

[21] Debates of the Constitutional Convention to Amend the Constitution of Pennsylvania, 1872-1873, at 190-91 (Harrisburg: State Office 1874).

[22] *Id.* at 212-18.

[23] *See Legislative Apportionments,* in PENNSYLVANIA CONSTITUTIONAL CONVENTION — 1967-1968, at 17 (1967) [hereinafter *Legislative Apportionments*].

new reapportionment scheme.[24] Moreover, the legislature quickly strayed from the constitutional mandate that it reapportion every ten years following the federal decennial census. This failure to reapportion allowed those legislators in power to maintain power. Thus, the legislature waited until 1887 (seven years after the next census) to reapportion again. No reapportionment at all took place after the 1910 census. The next redistricting occurred in 1921, following the 1920 census.[25] The legislature attempted to reapportion the House and Senate in 1937, but that legislation was subsequently invalidated by the courts and never resuscitated. In 1953, the House was successfully redistricted[26] but the Senate bill died because it omitted one township.[27] By the time the next reapportionment took place in 1966 — a reapportionment imposed by the Pennsylvania Supreme Court following the landmark decisions of *Baker v. Carr*[28] and *Reynolds v. Sims*[29] — the state senatorial districts in Pennsylvania had languished without a reapportionment for over four decades.

B. Revolutionary Changes in the 1960s

Pennsylvania was not alone in taking a lackadaisical approach to its own state constitutional reapportionment mandates. The overwhelming majority of state legislatures had dragged their heels, or refused entirely to reapportion, from 1901 through 1962. One commentator has noted that "[i]t is virtually impossible to find an example from 1901 to 1962, of an apportionment fairly and equitably performed which was voluntarily initiated by a state legislature ...."[30] The failure to reapportion became even more egregious as the United States became heavily industrialized, as the general population rose dramatically, as rural populations dwindled, and as urban areas boomed.[31] The result was rampant malapportionment. In Vermont, for instance, the most populous district in the state House of Representatives by the early 1960s contained 987 times more people than the least populous district.[32]

Similarly, serious problems haunted the legislative map-making process in Pennsylvania. The 1953 House reapportionment plan, for example, created a large number of multi-member districts that elected two, three or four representatives,

---

[24] FRANK B. EVANS, PENNSYLVANIA POLITICS, 1827-1877: A STUDY IN POLITICAL LEADERSHIP 99 (1966). The Republicans, who controlled the process, created districts which concentrated Democratic voters into single units, and diluted other Democratic areas by combining them with overwhelmingly Republican areas. HOBBS, *supra* note 2, at 14-15.

[25] *Legislative Apportionments, supra* note 23, at 17.

[26] The deciding vote on the House plan was cast by a hospitalized Republican who was wheeled into the chamber specifically for that purpose. HOBBS, *supra* note 2, at 16. The plan was later protested by Democrats, alleging partisan overtones. *Id.*

[27] *Id.* at 16. While the Senate and House were also redistricted in 1963, the Pennsylvania Supreme Court overturned this plan in 1964. *See infra* text accompanying notes 45-58.

[28] 369 U.S. 186 (1962).

[29] 377 U.S. 533 (1964).

[30] BOYD, CHANGING PATTERNS OF APPORTIONMENT 25 (1965), quoted in *Legislative Apportionments, supra* note 23, at 1.

[31] From 1860 to 1960, the population of the United States increased from 31.4 million to 179.3 million. James J. Hardy, *Metropolitan Reorganization*, 1966 UTAH L. REV. 517 (1966); *Legislative Apportionments, supra* note 23, at 1. During this same 100-year period, the percentage of people classified as "urban" jumped from 19.8% to 69.9%. *Id.*

[32] Robert B. McKay, *The Reapportionment Decisions: Retrospect and Prospect*, 51 A.B.A. J. 128, 130 (1965), quoted in *Legislative Apportionments, supra* note 23, at 1.

allowing skewed election results that greatly disfavored the minority political party.[33] Simultaneously, new population shifts were taking place from the cities to suburban areas, creating vast new pockets of malapportionment.[34]

In 1962, the U.S. Supreme Court handed down its landmark decision in *Baker v. Carr*,[35] holding for the first time that a state's failure to reapportion its own legislative districts raised a legitimate federal claim under the Equal Protection Clause of the Fourteenth Amendment.[36] The Court's opinion tacitly recognized that state reapportionment abuses might be leading to disenfranchisement of blacks and other minority voters crammed into underrepresented districts.

Two years later, the Court established the historic one-person-one-vote doctrine in an Alabama case where reapportionment had not occurred since 1901, despite a state constitutional provision mandating such redistricting.[37] In *Reynolds v. Sims*, population variances of as much as 41-to-1 existed in the Senate districts of Alabama, and ratios as great as 16-to-1 could be found in the House districts.[38] Chief Justice Earl Warren noted that "[l]egislators represent people, not trees or acres"[39] and condemned the reapportionment of Alabama's legislature as constitutionally intolerable:

> The right to vote freely for the candidate of one's choice is of the essence of a Democratic society, and any restrictions on that right strike at the heart of representative government. And the right of suffrage can be denied by a debasement or dilution of the weight of a citizen's vote just as effectively as by wholly prohibiting the free exercise of the franchise.[40]

The *Reynolds* Court adopted a somewhat pragmatic approach to cure this gross disparity among legislative districts and to preserve the sanctity of the right to vote. The Court held that the Equal Protection Clause of the Fourteenth Amendment required a state to make an honest and good faith effort to construct districts, in both houses of the legislature, as nearly equal in population as "practicable."[41] Divergence from strict parity in population would be acceptable so long as it did not dilute the one-person-one-vote precept in any significant way. Chief Justice Warren wrote that "[t]he overriding objective must be substantial equality of population among the various districts, so that the vote of any citizen is approximately equal in weight to that of any other citizen in the State."[42]

This statement explicitly recognized that mathematical exactness was not a constitutional requirement. Moreover, more flexibility was permissible with respect to state legislative apportionment schemes than with federal congressional districting. Preserving political subdivision lines (i.e. county, city and other boundaries) and designing "compact districts of contiguous territory" was a legitimate consideration in the drafting state legislative bodies as compared to Congress.[43] The *Rey-*

---

[33] HOBBS, *supra* note 2, at 16.

[34] *Id.* at 16-17.

[35] 369 U.S. 186 (1962).

[36] This was in contrast to the Supreme Court's previous decisions, which had concluded that issues of state reapportionment amounted to "political questions" not justifiable in the federal courts. *See* Colegrove v. Green, 328 U.S. 549 (1946).

[37] Reynolds v. Sims, 377 U.S. 533 (1964).

[38] *Id.* at 545.

[39] *Id.* at 562.

[40] *Id.* at 555.

[41] *Id.* at 577.

[42] *Id.* at 579.

[43] *Id.* at 577-79.

nolds Court thus expressly refused to construct any precise constitutional litmus test for evaluating state legislative apportionment schemes. Rather, challenges to state apportionment plans under the Fourteenth Amendment would have to await a case-by-case determination as this new era of political/constitutional history unfolded.[44]

C. Pennsylvania Seeks to Comply With Federal Law

Baker v. Carr and *Reynolds v. Sims* produced a swift impact throughout the United States as states scrambled to undo the blatantly malapportioned legislative districts that had been in place (in many instances) since the turn of the century. In Pennsylvania, the state legislature had tried, but failed, to enact a reapportionment bill following the 1960 census.[45] In March of 1962, a group of Pennsylvania voters sued the Secretary of the Commonwealth in an attempt to halt future elections of state legislators under existing apportionment statutes.[46] Although the Dauphin County court handling this lawsuit did not block the 1962 election, it did retain jurisdiction while it allowed the legislature to enact appropriate redistricting legislation.[47] During a special session in 1963, the General Assembly finally enacted two reapportionment statutes scheduled to become effective in January of 1964. The plaintiffs in the Dauphin County case therefore petitioned the Pennsylvania Supreme Court to take immediate jurisdiction before the 1964 elections. On September 29, 1964, the Pennsylvania Supreme Court issued a unanimous opinion in *Butcher v. Bloom* (I), authored by Justice Roberts. The Court held that the new Pennsylvania districts violated the one-person-one-vote standard of *Reynolds* and directed the legislature to prepare a new reapportionment plan before the 1966 election.[48]

When the Pennsylvania legislature failed to meet a September 1, 1965 deadline to properly reapportion the House and Senate, the Court itself set to work to reapportion the State. The Court invited proposals and maps from all interested parties and on February 4, 1966 unveiled the fruit of its efforts in *Butcher v. Bloom* (II),[49] a *per curiam* opinion issued in time for the primary elections to go forward. As the Court wrote in explaining those principles which had guided it:

> Our primary concern has been to provide for substantial equality of population among legislative districts. At the same time, we have sought to maintain the integrity of political subdivisions and to create compact districts of contiguous territory, insofar as these goals could be realized under the circumstances of the population distribution of

---

[44] *Id.* at 578.

[45] The failure resulted from partisan splits: the House maintained a 109 to 101 Democratic majority, but a 25 to 25 Democratic-Republican split existed in the Senate. The legislature did not succeed in enacting a reapportionment bill until Governor William Scranton called a special election in 1963. By that time, the legislature was again under Republican control, and *Baker v. Carr* had been handed down, throwing a wild card into the equation. *See* HOBBS, *supra* note 2, at 19.

[46] Butcher v. Trimarchi, 28 D. & C.2d 537 (Dauphin County 1962).

[47] *Id.*

[48] Butcher v. Bloom (I), 415 Pa. 438, 459-61, 203 A.2d 556, 568-69 (1964). The 1964 elections were permitted to proceed under the 1964 law, but the Court retained jurisdiction pending legislative action. In striking down the 1964 law as violative of the federal equal protection clause, the Pennsylvania Supreme Court noted that House districts ranged in population from 4, 485 to 81,534, while Senate districts ranged from 129,851 to 352,629 in population — far from the "substantial equality of population" required by *Reynolds. Id* at 448-456, 203 A.2d at 561-67.

[49] Butcher v. Bloom (II), 420 Pa. 305, 216 A.2d 457 (1966).

this Commonwealth. We believe such plans to be constitutionally valid and sound.[50]

Thus, the first watershed reapportionment in Pennsylvania after years of inertia and political volleying was accomplished by the Pennsylvania Supreme Court itself; seven jurists were forced to wade into the uncertain tangle of political district-making due to a recurring and unresolvable legislative gridlock.

Largely in response to this unsettling experience, the delegates to the Pennsylvania Constitutional Convention meeting in 1967-1968 immediately placed the revamping of the legislative reapportionment process on the agenda.[51] A Preparatory Committee headed by Lieutenant Governor Raymond J. Broderick appointed David Stahl (Solicitor of the city of Pittsburgh) to serve as Director of the Task Force on Legislative Apportionment. This Task Force produced a detailed publication for the benefit of Convention delegates exploring Pennsylvania's checkered history of redistricting and offered proposals for significant constitutional revamping.[52]

A number of divergent citizens groups expressed opinions to the Legislative Apportionment Task Force. The Americans for Democratic Action suggested that primary responsibility for reapportionment should remain in the hands of the legislature, with a commission to be appointed by the Governor only in the event that the legislature failed to act;[53] the League of Women Voters insisted on stringent timetables for reapportionment and hinted at the need for a special commission;[54] the AFL-CIO recommended that primary responsibility should lie with the legislature, but that strict guidelines be imposed;[55] and the Pennsylvania Bar Association agreed that the first opportunity to redistrict should remain in the legislature, subject, however, to immediate reapportionment by the Pennsylvania Supreme Court if the legislature failed to act.[56]

The Reapportionment Committee of the Convention ultimately proposed the creation of a hybrid commission dominated by legislators — the four leaders of the House and Senate — with the addition of one neutral chairman. In developing this structure, the Committee felt guided by the theory that "the appropriate group to make this change [i.e. redistricting] would be the legislature, because of the fact that they are more conversant with the State and also the legislative and senatorial districts and the method in which it should be divided in the best interests of the citizens of Pennsylvania."[57] At the same time, the Committee avoided the creation of a purely political body. The proposed commission represented a compromise between allowing the legislature as a body to reapportion itself, which had previously met with disaster, and taking the process entirely out of the hands of that body (i.e. the legislature) which possessed the greatest expertise for this task. If this new hybrid commission failed to enact a lawful reapportionment plan with-

---

[50] *Id.* at 309-10, 216 A.2d at 459.

[51] *See Legislative Apportionments, supra* note 23. Indeed the citizens of Pennsylvania themselves had made this a priority, by adopting the ballot question concerning the Constitutional Convention, which had as one of its stated purposes a revamping of the legislative reapportionment process.

[52] I DEBATES OF THE PENNSYLVANIA CONSTITUTIONAL CONVENTION OF 1967-1968, at 81 (daily journal Dec. 11, 1967) [hereinafter DEBATES]. *See also* §11, at 83 (History of Proposals).

[53] *See Legislative Apportionments, supra* note 23, at 91-93.

[54] *Id.* at 94-96.

[55] *Id.* at 101-04.

[56] *Id.* at 105-06.

[57] I DEBATES at 525 (daily journal Feb. 7, 1968) (remarks of Delegate Fagan).

in the prescribed time limits, the ultimate "tie-breaker" would be the Pennsylvania Supreme Court, just as it had been in 1964-1966.[58]

In the midst of the Convention, a proposed amendment emerged which would have permitted the General Assembly to *first* adopt a reapportionment plan of its own without the aid of a neutral chairman; only in the case of gridlock would a commission be created.[59] This amendment raised a hue and cry from a wide spectrum of delegates, who argued that the original idea of a commission was to "reliev[e] the legislators themselves of a very onerous duty; that in putting the burden of reapportionment in their lap, they were bound to be making enemies in even attempting to reapportion themselves, among their own members; that it was weakening their ability as legislators and was taking time that really they should not have been spending on it."[60] Delegate Baldridge charged that the legislators had never been able in the past to resist the temptation of apportioning themselves without regard to self-serving interests "because they were prejudiced judges and wanted to sit right on their own cases."[61] At the same time, a number of delegates expressed the concern that, even if a commission were utilized, there was a need to keep such political matters primarily out of the courts and within the jurisdiction of legislators.[62]

In the end, the proposal that a commission be created consisting of the majority and minority leaders of the House and Senate, along with one neutral chairman, prevailed. The committee's recommendations were adopted by the Convention with little dissent on February 29, 1968.[63] Constitutional amendments were overwhelmingly ratified by the voters of Pennsylvania, on April 23, 1968, by a vote of 1,063,603 to 583,091.[64] The result was a new Article II, Section 17 of the Pennsylvania Constitution.[65]

---

[58] *Id.* at 526.

[59] *Id.* at 562 (daily journal Feb. 8, 1968) (remarks of Delegate Shoemaker).

[60] *Id.* (remarks of Delegate Baldridge).

[61] *Id.* at 563 (remarks of Delegate Baldridge).

[62] As one delegate stated: "[W]e want to keep this out of the hands of the Supreme Court as much as possible." *Id.* (remarks of Delegate Ruth).

[63] *Id.* at 83.

[64] *Id.*

[65] For a complete text of Article II, Section 17 of the Pennsylvania Constitution, including minor revisions incorporated in 1981, *see* Appendix A.

III.
PENNSYLVANIA'S FIRST
REAPPORTIONMENT COMMISSIONS

A. The 1971 Reapportionment

In 1971, following the 1970 federal census, the newly constituted Pennsylvania Reapportionment Commission first tested its wings. As set forth in Article II, Section 17, the Commission was initially comprised of the majority and minority leaders of the House and Senate or their deputies. These consisted of Senate Majority Leader Thomas F. Lamb (D., Allegheny County), Senator Richard A. Tilghman (R., Montgomery County, deputized by Senate Minority Leader Robert D. Fleming (R., Allegheny County)); Majority Whip James Prendergast (D., Northampton County, deputized by House Majority Leader K. Leroy Irvis (D., Allegheny County)); and House Minority Leader Kenneth B. Lee (R., Sullivan County). The four partisan Commission members deadlocked immediately on the issue of who should serve as the fifth member and chairman. This decision was thus thrown to the Pennsylvania Supreme Court under the terms of Section 17(b) of the newly amended Pennsylvania Constitution. The Court selected Professor A. Leo Levin, a faculty member at the University of Pennsylvania Law School and a registered Democrat.[66]

Records of the inner-workings of the 1971 Pennsylvania Reapportionment Commission are spotty at best. It is clear that the Commission filed its preliminary reapportionment plan with the Secretary of the Commonwealth on November 17, 1971.[67] It is also clear that the Commission adopted several minor changes and filed its final reapportionment plan on December 29, 1971.[68] What happened otherwise is virtually impossible to decipher, as a result of lost and nonexistent records. One commentator observed years later that Chairman Levin emphasized mediation between the two political parties and cast few votes himself as tiebreaker, minimizing his role *qua* Chairman.[69] The brief minutes of the meetings indicate that the Commission met at least twelve times, usually in the Commission's tiny office in the basement of the Capitol.[70] There is no indication that these meetings were held in public (other than the vote on the Final Plan which was held in the Senate Caucus Room); indeed, it is doubtful that there was any spare space in the tiny Commission office for observers.

The minutes of the meetings also suggest that the Commission dealt with distinct chunks of the Pennsylvania map one at a time and voted on "mini-plans" relating to Philadelphia, Pittsburgh, and other regions separately. Here, Chairman

---

[66] HOBBS, *supra* note 2, at 24. Interestingly, aides to Democratic Governor Milton Shapp had charged that the Republicans had intentionally deadlocked the Commission and thrown the selection into the Pennsylvania Supreme Court, assuming that body (which maintained a 6-1 Republican majority) would appoint a Republican as chairman. The selection of Professor Levin belied this prediction. He was inactive politically. *Id.*

[67] Martin H. Belsky, *Reapportionment in the 1970's — A Pennsylvania Illustration*, 47 TEMP. L.Q. 3, 20 & n.125 (1973). *See also* Statement of A. Leo Levin, Chairman regarding Preliminary Plan and attached Fact Sheet (undated) (State Archives).

[68] *Id.* at 21-22 & nn.126-27.

[69] Sidney Wise, *Pennsylvania, in* REAPPORTIONMENT POLITICS: THE HISTORY OF REDISTRICTING IN THE 50 STATES 227-78 (Leroy Hardy et al. eds., 1981).

[70] *See* Minutes of the Legislative Reapportionment Commission (Apr. 21, 1971; May 12, 1971; July 13, 1971; Sept. 8, 1971; Sept. 27, 1971; Oct. 25, 1971; Oct. 26, 1971; Nov. 3, 1971; Nov. 16, 1971; Dec. 7, 1971; Dec. 27, 1971; Dec. 28, 1971) (State Archives).

Levin did act as tie-breaker. Although there is no record of specific votes, even on the preliminary or final plan, the minutes reflected key dissents to critical chunks of the map by the Republican Commission members (Senator Tilghman and Representative Lee). These suggest that the Republicans did not fully endorse the preliminary or final plans.[71]

As his closest advisor throughout the negotiations, Chairman Levin relied heavily on Thomas N. O'Neill, Jr., a partner in the prestigious Philadelphia law firm of Montgomery, McCracken, Walker & Rhoads. O'Neill had been appointed general counsel for the Commission at the time the preliminary reapportionment plan was filed. O'Neill's role appeared to have greatly diminished once a final plan was filed with the Secretary on December 29, 1971, at which time records of his involvement cease.

Eighteen parties appealed the Final Plan to the Pennsylvania Supreme Court, which scheduled oral arguments in Philadelphia *en masse* on February 2, 1972.[72] The bulk of the attacks focussed upon the city of Philadelphia and were launched by both partisan and nonpartisan challengers. The challengers principally contended that the districts were noncompact, failed to maintain the integrity of political subdivisions (including wards), placed undo emphasis on maintaining incumbency, and exceeded acceptable deviations in population.[73]

Interestingly, because the Constitution made no mention of who should represent the Commission in legal proceedings, the Attorney General of Pennsylvania, J. Shane Cramer, stepped into this role and filed a single brief in answer to all eighteen appeals.[74] The most vocal challenger to the Plan was Arlen Specter, then-District Attorney of Philadelphia, who contended that "[t]he Commission has butchered Philadelphia to prepare a feast for politicians!"[75] This charge notwithstanding, the Pennsylvania Supreme Court entered a brief *per curiam* order, based upon a 4-3 vote, on February 7, 1972, finding that the plan filed by the Legislative Reapportionment Commission "is in compliance with the mandates of the federal and Pennsylvania Constitutions and therefore shall have the force of law."[76]

It was not until June 5, 1972, that the Pennsylvania Supreme Court filed a full opinion explaining its decision upholding the plan. In *Commonwealth ex rel. Specter v. Levin*,[77] the four-justice majority began by blessing the new Commission format established by Article II, Section 17 of the Constitution. The Court observed that an even balance of Democratic and Republican leaders on the Commission "precludes the reapportionment process from being unfairly dominated by the party in power at the moment of apportionment."[78] Furthermore, the Court noted that the provision creating a neutral chairman to serve as tie-breaker "eliminates the possibility of a legislative deadlock on reapportionment such as the one that occurred in the legislature of this Commonwealth in 1965 and compelled this Court to undertake the task of reapportionment."[79]

---

[71] *Id.*

[72] Belsky, *supra* note 67, at 22. *See also State Redistricting Plan Hit by 18 Before Top Court*, HARRISBURG EVENING NEWS, Feb. 3, 1972.

[73] Belsky, *supra* note 67, at 22-23.

[74] *Id.* at 23.

[75] *Id.* at 22 n.132.

[76] Commonwealth *ex rel.* Specter v. Levin, 448 Pa. 1, 4-5 (1972) (order per curiam), *appeal dismissed sub nom.* Specter v. Tucker, 409 U.S. 810 (1972).

[77] 448 Pa. 1, 293 A.2d 15 (1972).

[78] *Id.* at 6, 293, A.2d at 17.

[79] *Id.* at 6-7, 293 A.2d at 17.

Relying on the command of *Reynolds* that the "overriding objective" of any plan must be "substantial equality of population among the various districts,"[80] the Court next addressed the issue of numerical equality. In a series of cases after *Reynolds*, the U.S. Supreme Court had rejected rigid mathematical standards for assessing substantial population equality. The *Specter* Court therefore held that the population deviations presented in the House and Senate reapportionment plans were acceptable. The Final Plan had resulted in a maximum deviation range of 4.31% in Senate districts and 5.46% in House districts. Forty of the Senate districts deviated less than 1.5% from the ideal; 149 of the House districts deviated less than 1.5% from the ideal.[81] Indeed, the Court stated that no decision of the United States or Pennsylvania Supreme Court had ever invalidated a reapportionment plan exhibiting population deviations as minimal as these and concluded "that the deviations clearly do not dilute the equal-population principle 'in any significant way.'"[82]

Satisfied that the Commission's plan fully achieved the overriding objective of "substantial equality of population," the Court then turned to the secondary goals of maintaining the integrity of the political subdivisions and providing for contiguous and compact districts, as required by Article II, Section 16 of the Pennsylvania Constitution.[83] The Court acknowledged that because the primary goal of reapportionment was substantial population equality, a certain amount of fragmentation of political subdivisions was inevitable. The Court then gave positive reviews to the Commission's plan, which divided 74.6% of the state's counties into the ideal number of senate districts while dividing only 25.4% of the counties into more than the ideal number of senate districts. This feature of the plan, wrote the Court, was sufficiently sensitive to the requirement of maintaining political boundaries to pass constitutional muster.[84]

Additionally, the *Specter* majority easily concluded that the Commission's plan satisfied contiguity requirements because no part of any district was physically separate from any other part of that district. The Court conceded that any reapportionment plan would contain a certain degree of "unavoidable non-compactness" due to the unevenness of population density, but the Court also held that the mere fact certain districts appeared to be noncompact when one examined an electoral map did not mean that the configurations were constitutionally unacceptable. Since none of the challengers had offered any concrete data to demonstrate an unacceptable level of non-compactness, the Court held that the Commission's plan was lawful.[85]

Chief Justice Jones, Justice Pomeroy and Justice Manderino dissented, blasting the Commission's plan because of the high levels of population variances

---

[80] *Id.* at 7, 293 A.2d at 18.

[81] *Id.* at 15-16, 293 A.2d at 22. The percentage "deviation" refers to the maximum spread from the smallest district in the House or Senate, to the largest district. An "ideal" district can be hypothesized based upon absolute numerical equality among the districts, once one knows the total population of the Commonwealth from the census. The "deviation" is another way of qualifying the total span — in both a "plus" and "minus" direction — between the ideal district and the actual districts created by reapportionment.

[82] *Id.* at 16, 293 A.2d at 22, *quoting Reynolds.*

[83] As mentioned earlier, the "compact and contiguous" language dated back to earlier Constitutions, in the context of districts created after cities or counties were split. *See* discussions of PA. CONST. of 1873, *supra* notes 16-24 and accompanying text.

[84] *Specter,* 448 Pa. at 16-17, 293 A.2d at 22-23.

[85] *Id.* at 17-19, 293 A.2d at 23-24.

it tolerated.[86] The dissenters also viewed with disfavor the lack of compactness of the districts. Chief Justice Jones invoked the Chinese proverb "'[o]ne picture is worth more than 10,000 words," and asserted that the districts "twist and wind their way across the map in an erratic, amorphous fashion ...."'[87] Justice Pomeroy chastised the Commission for presenting the finished plan in a vacuum of silence. Without an explanation of the Commission's reasoning or motives in allowing for certain population deviations and splits of municipalities, he wrote, it was impossible to judge the plan's lawfulness and assess the Commission's reasons for rejecting the exceptions to the plan filed by concerned citizens.[88]

Despite these objections to what can at best be described as an experimental venture into reapportionment by the new Commission, the plan withstood constitutional attack and, for the first time in the history of Pennsylvania, a quasi-legislative bipartisan body of five individuals succeeded in reapportioning the Commonwealth.

B. The 1981 Reapportionment

Ten years later, a newly constituted Commission took a fresh stab at drawing districts based upon a decade's worth of federal and state reapportionment precedent. The initial Commission members consisted of Senate Majority Leader Robert C. Jubelirer (R., Blair County); Senate Minority Leader Edward P. Zemprelli (D., Allegheny County); House Majority Leader Samuel E. Hayes (R., Blair County); and House Minority Whip James J. Manderino (D., Westmoreland County, deputized by House Minority Leader K. Leroy Irvis (D., Allegheny County)). The selection of a chairman in 1981 was complicated by the fact that a vacancy had occurred on the Pennsylvania Supreme Court (which then consisted of three Democrats and three Republicans) with Governor Richard Thornburgh nominating Commonwealth Court Judge Roy Wilkinson Jr., a Republican, to fill the empty seat. Democrats refused to contribute any of the thirty-four votes needed for Wilkinson's confirmation until they were sure that the reapportionment chairman would be someone acceptable to them; the Democrats feared that the selection of a chairman might otherwise be thrown to a Republican-dominated Court.[89] After holding the appointment of Judge Wilkinson "hostage" for some time, the Democrats finally agreed with their Republican colleagues on the selection of James O. Freedman, Dean of the University of Pennsylvania Law School, to serve as Chairman of the Reapportionment Commission. The vote in favor of Dean Freedman was unanimous.[90]

Thomas N. O'Neill, Jr., who would later become a federal judge in Philadelphia, was selected to serve as counsel to the Commission for a second time, at a rate of $135 per hour plus expenses.[91] Chairman Freedman was paid a *per diem* of

---

[86] Id. at 22, 293 A.2d at 25-26 (Jones, C.J., dissenting); 448 Pa. at 25-26, 293 A.2d at 27 (Pomeroy, J., dissenting); 448 Pa. at 29, 293 A.2d at 29 (Manderino, J., dissenting), see Bloom (II), 420 Pa. 305, 216 A.2d 457 (1966).

[87] Id. at 21-22, 293 A.2d at 25 (quoting Reock, Jr., Measuring Compactness as a Requirement of Legislative Apportionment, 5 MIDWEST J. OF POL. SCI. 70 (1961)) (Jones, C.J., dissenting).

[88] Id. at 25-26, 293 A.2d at 27 (Pomeroy, J., dissenting).

[89] See Carmen Bruto, The Redistricting Game, THE HARRISBURG PATRIOT, Mar. 9, 1981; Peter Cohellos, Law School Dean Heads Group to Redraw Legislative Districts, THE DAILY PENNSYLVANIAN, Feb. 27, 1981.

[90] Minutes of the Legislative Reapportionment Commission (Feb. 23, 1981) (State Archives).

[91] John Scotzin, Redistricting Panel Ends up With $159,693 Left Over, THE EVENING NEWS (Harrisburg), Jan. 1, 1983.

$200 per day, as of the date of his appointment.[92] The Commission established a budget of $380,000.[93]

Once again, the precise workings of the 1981 Commission remain shrouded in mystery and lost paperwork. Although the Commission apparently held twelve public meetings from the time of its inception until the vote on a final plan,[94] transcripts exist for only three of them. A preliminary plan was unanimously approved by the Commission on August 20, 1981.[95] A public hearing was held on September 24, 1981, at which the Commission heard testimony from more than sixty witnesses.[96] After making "numerous changes" to the preliminary plan based upon testimony and written exceptions, the Commission unanimously adopted a Final Plan on October 13, 1981.[97]

Little survives in the minutes or transcripts to provide a close view of the influence of Chairman Freedman on the Commission. Much of the work of Commission members and staffs, as is usual for such a body, occurred behind closed doors. Public meetings were held more to hear witnesses and seal compromises than to air debate; consequently, there is little to serve as a signature of Freedman's style. It is clear that Chairman Freedman was well respected by the Commission members and swiftly got the process off dead center by establishing percentages of population deviations within which the staffs had to operate (4% for the House, and 2% for the Senate).[98] It is also clear that the Commission's counsel, Thomas O'Neill, was heavily influential in the process, sitting at the chairman's side throughout most negotiations between Democrats and Republicans.[99] Other than these salient facts, documents provide little trace of the internal workings of the Commission up to the time it filed its final bipartisan plan in October of 1981.

As in the case of the 1971 reapportionment, the Pennsylvania Supreme Court held argument simultaneously on all twenty-nine objections to the Final Plan on December 7, 1981. The Commission, this time, was represented by its own legal counsel, Thomas O'Neill, rather than by the state Attorney General, as had been the approach in 1971. On December 29, 1981, the Court upheld the Commission's map in *In re Reapportionment Plan*[100] and thereafter denied ten applications for reargument. As in the *Specter* case a decade earlier, the majority of the Court concluded that the goal of substantial equality in population was paramount and that "if need be, the concerns for compactness and adherence to political subdivision lines must yield to this 'overriding objective.'"[101] Justice Roberts, writing for the majority, noted that the 1982 Plan was more precise than its predecessor. The spread of "population deviation" between senate districts was only 1.9%, and the deviation in the House from the ideal district was only 2.8%. Thus, according to the Court, "the final plan achieves an equality of population among legislative dis-

---

[92] Minutes of the Legislative Reapportionment Commission (Mar. 16, 1981) (State Archives).
[93] Scotzin, *supra* note 91.
[94] *See* Minutes of the Legislative Reapportionment Commission (Oct. 13, 1981) (State Archives).
[95] Minutes of the Legislative Reapportionment Commission (Aug. 20, 1981) (State Archives).
[96] Minutes of the Legislative Reapportionment Commission (Sept. 24, 1981) (State Archives).
[97] Minutes of the Legislative Reapportionment Commission (Oct. 13, 1981) (State Archives).
[98] Interview with 1981 Legislative Reapportionment Commission staff.
[99] *Id.*
[100] 497 Pa. 525, 442 A.2d 661 (1981).
[101] *Id.* at 535, 442 A.2d at 666 (quoting Commonwealth *ex rel.* Specter v. Levin, 448 Pa. 1, 13, 293 A.2d 15, 21 (1972), *appeal dismissed sub nom.* Specter v. Tucker, 409 U.S. 810 (1972)).

tricts closer to the constitutional ideal of 'one person, one vote' than any previous reapportionment plan in the history of the Commonwealth."[102]

Furthermore, the majority concluded that the Commission had not impermissibly divided counties and municipalities in fashioning its reapportionment scheme. Of the 67 counties and 2,569 municipalities in the Commonwealth, the Senate plan had preserved the boundaries of 41 counties and all but 2 municipalities. With respect to the House districts, the plan had maintained the boundaries of 19 counties and all but 87 municipalities. Thus, the Court concluded that the 1981 plan compared favorably to the 1971 plan in the "splits" department.[103] Reading the constitutional language of Article II, Section 17 as a sort of presumption in favor of the Commission, the majority found that the appellants had failed to sustain their burden of demonstrating "'that the final plan is contrary to law.'"[104]

The dissenters, Justices Nix, Kauffman and Larsen, were less vehement than those who took issue with the Plan in the previous decade. Justice Nix concluded that the Final Plan had sacrificed too much in order to accomplish population equality and went too far in dividing counties and municipalities. He further contended that the Plan had not paid sufficient attention to "communities of interest" (particularly in Philadelphia), thus violating the requirements of contiguousness and compactness.[105] Justice Larsen objected that the Plan had achieved population equality at the expense of the integrity of the State's political subdivisions.[106] Finally, Justice Kauffman warned against the Court acting as a mere "rubber stamp" for the Commission and echoed the concerns of Justice Pomeroy a decade earlier in chiding the Commission for providing no explanation or justification for the way in which it had arrived at a Plan.[107] Justice Kauffman further took the position that the Court should not sustain the Final Plan without some evidence demonstrating that the Commission had fully considered and implemented all of the constitutionally-mandated reapportionment standards, including those contained in Article II, Section 16 of the Pennsylvania Constitution relating to compactness, contiguousness, and sanctity of political boundaries. The Plan should be upheld, Justice Kauffman argued, only if these factors had been considered to the fullest extent possible consistent with the dominant objective of achieving population equality.[108]

A brief scandal surfaced when *The Philadelphia Inquirer* reported that Justice Rolf Larsen, a Democrat, had promised key Democratic political leaders that he would favor "Democratic interests" in any legislative reapportionment cases that would come before him.[109] After this flap passed, however, the reapportionment process was quickly put to rest. No appeals were taken to the United States Supreme Court.

After the 1981 Commission-driven reapportionment plan received the Pennsylvania Supreme Court's stamp of approval, albeit over a certain cloud of dissent,

---

[102] *Id.* at 534, 442 A.2d at 665-66.
[103] *Id.* at 538-39, 442 A.2d at 668-69.
[104] *Id.* at 531, 442 A.2d at 664 (quoting Commonwealth *ex rel.* Specter v. Levin, 448 Pa. at 19, 293 A.2d at 24).
[105] *Id.* at 540-41, 442 A.2d at 669 (Nix, J., dissenting).
[106] *Id.* at 542, 442 A.2d at 669-70 (Larsen, J., dissenting).
[107] *Id.* at 548-50, 442 A.2d at 672-74 (Kauffman, J., dissenting).
[108] *Id.*
[109] *See* Daniel R. Biddle, *A Matter of Ethics: Justice Larsen and friends,* THE PHILADELPHIA INQUIRER, May 17, 1981.

several generalizations could be drawn. First, in the wake of *Baker v. Carr* and *Reynolds v. Sims* in the early 1960s, the overriding concern of the first two Commissions was population equality, almost to the exclusion of all other factors. The 1971 and the 1981 Commissions had placed enormous emphasis (as a first critical step) upon arriving at an "acceptable" population deviation figure that would be tolerated in the House and Senate districts. Once the Chairman lent his blessing to an acceptable percentage, based upon prevailing court decisions, the political party leaders on the Commission were then generally free to work out political compromises on the configurations of the districts themselves, with "red alert" warnings being sounded on such issues as compactness and splits of political boundaries only in the case of extreme departures from the Pennsylvania Constitution.

Second, the Pennsylvania Supreme Court tacitly approved of this superemphasis on population equality at the expense of other factors, recognizing that it was impossible to draw a jigsaw puzzle containing equal-sized pieces without sacrificing a certain degree of aesthetic beauty and neat line-drawing. Likewise, having drawn the reapportionment plan itself in 1966, the Court was sensitive to the fact that, unless absolutely necessary, it was not the Court's business, nor its desire, to plunge into this legislative exercise. Reapportionment was inherently a political process; the Constitution itself had created a Commission comprised of the political party leaders from the House and the Senate. Thus, a certain amount of horse-trading and mutually agreeable "gerrymandering" was not only inevitable, but had some merit. The Court would not soil its hands in the politics of reapportionment unless absolutely necessary.

Finally, through the mouths of the dissenters it became evident that one built-in weak spot in the Commission mechanism was that no guidepost existed as to what record, if any, the Commission was required to provide the Court in articulating or justifying its decision-making. The majority opinions in both 1972 and 1982 accepted the plans "on their faces," rendering decisions as to lawfulness without any meaningful record regarding the internal tickings of the Commission. Equality of population was the big-ticket item, and, once the Court was satisfied on this score, a presumption seemed to flow in favor of the Commission on all other matters, absent some gross abuse.

The dissenters in both 1972 and 1982, on the other hand, seemed to want an affirmative justification each time the Commission tread into an area roughly governed by Article II, Section 16 of the Pennsylvania Constitution. Where a challenger alleged that map-making could have been accomplished more artfully, at less expense to the "secondary" mandates of the Constitution — compactness, contiguity, integrity of political boundaries — the dissenters remained unsatisfied with a silent record. They voiced a willingness to strike down the Reapportionment Plan unless the Commission could affirmatively establish that such sacrifices were "absolutely necessary."[110]

The gradual preeminence of the one-person-one-vote principle in the 1971 and 1981 reapportionments would be turned on its head in the reapportionment of 1991. By this time, computers and high technology would make equality in population a simple exercise, while new frontiers, particularly the Federal Voting Rights Act of 1965[111] (as it had been amended in 1982), would loom up with historic prominence and threaten to topple reapportionment plans in Pennsylvania and across the nation.

---

[110] *See* PA. CONST. art. II, §16.
[111] 42 U.S.C. §§1971-1974(e) (1982).

IV.
THE REAPPORTIONMENT OF 1991

A. Setting Up the Commission

The federal decennial census of 1990, conducted by the Department of Commerce and its Bureau of Census in nine months pursuant to the directive of Congress,[112] catapulted the 1991 Pennsylvania reapportionment into motion. Federal and state law contemplated that reapportionment would not actually begin until the Secretary of Commerce issued a report setting forth the census data in "usable form,"[113] a form that could actually be used by state reapportioning bodies. Although this did not occur until midsummer of 1991, Pennsylvania (like most states) took steps to set the process in motion much earlier.

On March 13, 1991, Senate Majority Leader F. Joseph Loeper (R., Delaware County) called the first organizational meeting of the Legislative Reapportionment Commission in the State Capitol. Pursuant to Article II, Section 17(b) of the Pennsylvania Constitution, the four "political" members of the Commission consisted of Senator Loeper (selected as Temporary Chairman); Senate Minority Leader Robert J. Mellow (D., Lackawanna County); House Majority Leader H. William DeWeese (D., Greene County); and Representative John M. Perzel (R., Philadelphia, deputized by House Minority Leader Representative Matthew J. Ryan (R., Delaware County)).[114] The Temporary Commission adopted a resolution to solicit letters of interest from persons wishing to be candidates for the position of chairman. The resolution was circulated in the *Pennsylvania Bulletin* and to the deans of all Pennsylvania law schools.

On April 3, 1991, the Temporary Commission met in the State Capitol to interview candidates who had expressed an interest in the chairmanship. These included Arlin M. Adams, Retired Judge of the U.S. Court of Appeals for the Third Circuit, Associate Dean John L. Gedid of the Widener University School of Law in Harrisburg, Dean Mark A. Nordenberg of the University of Pittsburgh School of Law, and Dean John A. Maher of the Dickinson School of Law, as well as a half dozen attorneys and private citizens.[115]

Dissension erupted within the tentative Commission on April 8, 1991, the date originally set for a final vote on the chairman. Senator Loeper and Representative Perzel (the Republican members of the Commission) voted to appoint Dean Mark Nordenberg as Chairman, while Representative DeWeese voted against his appointment and Senator Mellow (the second Democrat) abstained, requesting that other nominees be considered before a vote was taken.[116] The Temporary Commission was unable to reach agreement on several other nominees, and a brief recess was held. When the Commission members returned, Representative Perzel took the position that a quorum had been present and that a majority of the Commission had voted in favor of Dean Nordenberg, since the vote was two in the affirmative, one in the negative, and one abstention. Senator Loeper concurred in this in-

---

[112] *See* 13 U.S.C. §141(a), (b) (1983).

[113] *See* 13 U.S.C. §141(c) (1983); PA. CONST. art. II, §17(c).

[114] *See* Minutes of the Legislative Reapportionment Commission (Mar. 13, 1991) (State Archives).

[115] *See* Transcript of the Legislative Reapportionment Commission Meeting (Apr. 3, 1991) (State Archives).

[116] *See* Transcript of the Legislative Reapportionment Commission Meeting 4-5 (Apr. 8, 1991) (State Archives).

terpretation of the voting. The two Democratic members vigorously disagreed.[117] This led to a disharmonious adjournment.

On April 8, 1991 (that same day), Senator Loeper as Temporary Chairman submitted the name of Dean Mark A. Nordenberg to the Secretary of the Commonwealth as the individual selected to serve as Chairman of the Commission.[118] The Secretary replied on April 9, 1991, that the name of Dean Nordenberg lacked sufficient votes to constitute the selection of the Commission[119] and would not be accepted. Uncomfortable with his position in the political crossfire, Dean Nordenberg withdrew his name as a candidate for the position on April 12th, expressing a desire to avoid controversy and needless litigation which would delay the Commission's important work.[120]

When the Temporary Commission reconvened on April 23, 1991, to cast a new vote on the chairman, the two Democratic Commission members were conspicuously absent. A quorum could not be reached.[121] Further attempts to arrange a suitable time for the Commission to meet prior to the constitutional deadline failed. The selection of a chairman was thus thrown to the Pennsylvania Supreme Court under the terms of Article II, Section 17(b) of the Pennsylvania Constitution.[122]

On May 6, 1991, the Pennsylvania Supreme Court appointed Pittsburgh attorney, Robert J. Cindrich, to serve as Chairman.[123] Cindrich, a registered Democrat, had earned a reputation for fairness and adherence to constitutional principle when he served under President Jimmy Carter as the U.S. Attorney for the Western District of Pennsylvania. He had also served in a variety of other positions in government and public service throughout his career.

Chairman Cindrich called the first meeting of the fully-constituted Commission on June 11, 1991. At this time he expressed his intention to serve in a "neutral" fashion and to develop a consensus plan working with the political leaders of both parties.[124] The four political members of the Commission expressed their confidence in the competence and impartiality of the judicially-selected Chairman.[125]

Thus, just as in 1972, the political leaders' inability to agree upon a nonpolitical chairman had cast this important decision to the Pennsylvania Supreme Court. For the first time, however, the job fell upon an individual other than an academician, a practicing attorney who would take a more active role in the process than any past chairman.

---

[117] *Id.* at 15-19.

[118] *See* Letter from Secretary Christopher A. Lewis to Senator F. Joseph Loeper (Apr. 9, 1991) (State Archives).

[119] *Id.*

[120] *See* Transcript of the Legislative Reapportionment Commission Meeting 2 (Apr. 23, 1991) (State Archives); *see also* letter from Nordenberg to Loeper dated April 12, 1991 (State Archives).

[121] *Id.* at 1-3.

[122] The Constitution provides that no later than 60 days following the official reporting of the federal decennial census, the four "political" members of the Commission shall be certified to the Secretary of the Commonwealth. Within 45 days after this certification, the four members are required to select a chairman and certify his or her name immediately to the Secretary; otherwise a majority of the Supreme Court is required to select a chairman within 30 days thereafter. *See* PA. CONST. art. II, §17(b).

[123] *See In re:* Appointment of Chairman of the Legislative Reapportionment Commission, Judicial Administration Docket No. 105A (May 6, 1991) (State Archives).

[124] Transcript of the Legislative Reapportionment Commission Meeting 2-5 (June 11, 1991) (State Archives).

[125] *Id.* at 5-10.

B. Administrative Tasks of the Commission

The first order of administrative business was addressed at the meeting of June 11, 1991, at which Chairman Cindrich nominated individuals for the positions of Chief Counsel and Executive Director, both of whom were unanimously approved. To serve as Chief Counsel, the Chairman named Stephen J. Harmelin, Esquire, a highly-respected attorney and senior partner at the Philadelphia firm of Dilworth, Paxson, Kalish & Kauffman. Attorney Harmelin, although a registered Republican, had served as a White House aide in the administration of President Lyndon B. Johnson as well as on the boards of a host of prestigious corporations and professional committees.[126] To serve as Executive Director, Chairman Cindrich nominated Ken Gormley, an attorney practicing at the firm of Mansmann Cindrich & Titus in Pittsburgh. Gormley also served as an adjunct professor on the faculty at the University of Pittsburgh School of Law, where he taught and specialized in state constitutional law.[127] Although the Pennsylvania Constitution was silent as to what staff the Chairman was entitled to appoint and what personnel the Commission as a body might hire, these decisions (like many throughout the process) were ultimately left to the Chairman's sound judgment and improvisation as the process unfolded.

The Constitution was equally silent as to the actual mechanics of the Commission's operation. At the organizational meeting of the Commission on July 17, 1991, the Chairman introduced, and the full Commission approved, a host of resolutions dealing with administrative matters. At this meeting, Representative Allen G. Kukovich (D., Westmoreland County) was deputized to serve in place of Representative H. William DeWeese on behalf of the House Democrats, putting in place the five members of the Commission who would ultimately serve and vote throughout the balance of the reapportionment work. Somewhat informally, it was decided that the Commission should establish an office in the Capitol building (rather than further afield) to ensure central access to staff and documents. Space was located in Room 612 of the North Office Building, a particularly suitable venue because it was located in a nonpartisan, "neutral" wing of the Capitol.

The Commission then approved Resolution 2A, naming as Executive Secretary Barbara Butterfield and establishing salaries for staff members.[128] Barbara Butterfield was a highly qualified professional "on loan" from the staff of a senior member of the House, specifically selected because of her experience with both House and Senate staffers and the inner-workings of both legislative bodies. This appointment was considered critical because the Chairman and Executive Director had little familiarity with the personnel within the Capitol. Moreover, a reliable manager of the office in Harrisburg was required since the Chairman and Executive Director would spend a great deal of time in their own offices in Pittsburgh.

A budget of $500,000.00 was established for the Commission, in addition to $159,963.90 remaining from the legislative reapportionment of 1981, for a total budget of $659,963.90.[129] The Chairman's *per diem* was set at $300 for each day he expended a "significant or substantial" amount of time on Commission business,

---

[126] *Id.* at 23-26.
[127] *Id.* at 33-35.
[128] Transcript of the Legislative Reapportionment Commission Meeting 5 (June 11, 1991) (State Archives).
[129] *Id.* at 6; Resolution #2G.

whether in Harrisburg or elsewhere.[130] For the sake of convenience and uniformity, the existing 1991 Financial Operating Rules of the Senate were adopted *in toto* to govern expenses, personnel policies, and other administrative matters.[131] This meant, as a practical matter, that all financial processings and disbursements would take place through the chief clerk of the senate, Gary Crowell. This arrangement proved to be extremely satisfactory because the chief clerk had already developed a high level of expertise in such matters and because the Commission could simply tap into the existing procedures and personnel rather than inventing its own guidelines under the sharp time constraints of the reapportionment process.

In reality, much of the early work of the Commission in organizing itself was accomplished through informal cooperation among the Democrat and Republican staffs of the House and Senate. Potentially cumbersome details such as obtaining equipment for the office, establishing internal operating procedures for the Commission, and finding messengers and other clerical assistance were often resolved through phone calls and mutual agreement rather than spending unnecessary taxpayer funds on "purchasing" such goods and services from outside sources. This sort of unscripted cooperation was extremely important because it allowed the Chairman and Executive Director to devote the bulk of their early time to actual reapportionment work, since the 90-day clock established by the Constitution to achieve a preliminary plan had already begun to tick.[132] A highly qualified research assistant, Daniel Cooper (a graduate of Princeton who had been accepted to Harvard Law School) was hired for the summer to carry out legal research. This work began immediately.

The 1991 Commission had, at best, thin historical documentation to guide it. Other than the bulky and inaccessible materials kept in the state archives, the only records of the 1981 and 1971 reapportionments were an informal collection of boxes housed by the Executive Director of the Legislative Data Processing Center. LDPC, as that entity is known in the Capitol, is a highly sophisticated non-partisan office responsible for collecting and tabulating data on a host of projects for the House and Senate. Although the reapportionment records preserved by LDPC were of limited usefulness because they were incomplete, the records proved to be the only centralized source of information during the reapportionment project. The only "institutional memory" of the Commission was Al Stockslager, the Executive Director of LDPC, who had been actively involved in the 1981 reapportionment and had kept personal files. As a result, LDPC proved to be critical in assisting the staffs as well as the Chairman of the 1991 Commission. As will be discussed, LDPC is likely to continue to grow in importance as the Commonwealth confronts future reapportionments.

C. Threshold Legal Issues

Before beginning the task of reapportioning the legislative districts within the Commonwealth, the Commission faced a number of threshold legal issues which, by virtue of the Constitution, had to be addressed immediately. Foremost among these was determining when the census data was "usable" such that the Commission could rely upon it and go forward.

Article II, Section 17(c) of the Pennsylvania Constitution provides:

---

[130] *Id.* at 10; Resolution #2B.
[131] *Id.* at 7; Resolution #2C.
[132] *See* PA. CONST. art. II, §17(c).

> No later than ninety days after either the commission has been duly certified or the population data for the Commonwealth as determined by the federal decennial census are available, whichever is later in time, the commission shall file a preliminary reapportionment plan with such elections officer.

Thus, the magic clock would begin to tick as of the date the federal census data was deemed "available" to the Commission. The Commission would then have 90 days in which to file a preliminary reapportionment plan; failing to do so, the process would be thrown into the hands of the Pennsylvania Supreme Court under the terms of Section 17(g), absent an extension for cause shown. Thus, determining when the census data could be deemed "usable" was a critical threshold determination. In theory, if the Commission were to miscalculate the 90-day deadline by even a single day, it could lose jurisdiction and forfeit the entire process to the courts.

With this hazard in mind, the Commission's first assignment to its Chief Counsel, Stephen Harmelin, was to render a legal opinion as to the "usability" of the census data. The issue was anything but clear-cut. Although LDPC had received raw data from the U.S. Census Bureau on February 22, 1991, it was subsequently determined that the data was inaccurate in a host of respects.[133] Population data was faulty at the precinct level due to problems with "split blocks." Additionally, although certain precinct boundaries within the Commonwealth had changed, the federal census data failed to reflect these changes. Finally, LDPC discovered coding errors in the Census Bureau data, further skewing the population figures.[134] All of these errors required LDPC to make adjustments and corrections before delivering the data to the Commission, which did not occur until June 27, 1991, the date on which the revised data was delivered to Chairman Cindrich.[135] It was not until these changes were made, according to the testimony of Mr. Stockslager, that the Commission could "meaningfully draw both House and Senate districts."[136] Even after these major revisions, additional changes and "fine-tunings" would take place.

In 1981, the Pennsylvania Supreme Court had been forced to confront that same issue, but failed to resolve it directly. In that year, the individual members of the Legislative Reapportionment Commission had petitioned the Court to exercise extraordinary jurisdiction and render a declaratory judgment as to whether the population data was "available" within the meaning of the Constitution when it was actually transmitted in raw form by the federal government to the state; alternatively, the Commission suggested the data was "available" when it had been translated by LDPC into a form that was actually usable. On March 26, 1981, the Chief Justice of the Pennsylvania Supreme Court issued an order stating that the 90-day period within which the Commission was required to file a preliminary plan began to run on the date that the Commission received the population data from the federal decennial census *"in usable form* (breakdown of data by precinct and ward)."[137]

---

[133] *See* Transcript of the Legislative Reapportionment Commission Meeting 16-22 (July 17, 1991) (State Archives).

[134] *Id.* at 19-22.

[135] *Id.* at 21-22.

[136] *Id.* at 21.

[137] *See* Memorandum from Barbara A. Brown, Esq. to Stephen J. Harmelin, Esq. (July 11, 1991) (State Archives).

The term "usable form," as coined by the state's highest court, provided at least a guidepost for the Commission in 1991. But a number of Commission members urged that a declaratory judgment action should be filed with the Pennsylvania Supreme Court, requesting a specific ruling as to the date on which the data was "usable."[138] Other members objected; this approach would prompt delays. Chief Counsel Harmelin believed that the issue of usability "is really a factual determination to be made by this Commission based upon all the information available to it" and that there existed a "range of availability and usable form."[139] Given the conclusion by LDPC that the data was really not usable until it was revised and delivered to the Chairman on June 27th, Chief Counsel Harmelin felt that the Commission should make this factual determination itself and move forward, without involving the courts.[140]

In the end, the Commission voted to forego a declaratory judgment action and reached its own determination that the data was "usable" as of June 27, 1991, the date the errors in the raw federal data had been corrected by LDPC.[141] In hindsight, this decision was quite prudent. The Pennsylvania Supreme Court is hardly in a position to jump into reapportionment matters each decade, without warning, and begin reviewing factual determinations on such short notice. The Commission was in the best position to manage its own calendar and reach findings of fact on issues that directly affected its own business, particularly the "usability" question. Absent a clearly erroneous, bad faith decision in this regard, it is hard to imagine that the Pennsylvania Supreme Court would (or should) upset the Commission's determination on this score. Indeed, the "usability" issue quickly became moot in the 1991 experience, a fitting conclusion to a relatively picayune matter.

A related issue arose in 1991 which will raise interesting questions for future Commissions. Representative John Perzel expressed concern that LDPC had not provided data broken down by race and voting age population, which was essential to the Commission drawing districts in compliance with the Federal Voting Rights Act.[142] In Representative Perzel's view, "if we don't have the racial breakdown, then it's not in usable form."[143] The Executive Director of LDPC indicated that such racial data would be available shortly to the Commission. The Chairman and Chief Counsel were reluctant to conclude that the "usability" of data should be determined on this ground alone; the Commission could at least begin its task while awaiting the racial breakdowns.[144] Given the experience of the 1991 Commission, and the growing importance of access to information by all citizens, it is difficult to comprehend how federal census data can be truly "usable" for modern reapportionment purposes without accompanying racial data. For that reason, racial data should be included in the first round of data released to the Commission in future years. But due to the press of business in 1991, and the relative novelty of such Voting Rights Act questions, the process moved forward.

---

[138] Transcript of the Legislative Reapportionment Commission Meeting 37-46 (July 17, 1991) (State Archives).
[139] *Id.* at 14.
[140] *Id.* at 43-44.
[141] *Id.* at 46.
[142] *Id.* at 22-24.
[143] *Id.* at 24.
[144] *Id.* at 24-26.

V.
THE FUNCTIONING OF THE 1991 COMMISSION

Little has been written about the inner-workings of the Legislative Reapportionment Commission in Pennsylvania. Consequently, little is known by citizens, potential litigants, the courts, and even lawmakers about its operation.

Until recently, all map-making and line-drawing was accomplished according to the old-fashioned method: with pencils, maps of the Commonwealth, and scraps of paper to calculate population for proposed districts. By 1991, this antiquated process had changed dramatically. Sophisticated computer systems and software were already in place for nearly two years before a Chairman was named to the Commission in 1991. No centralized computer had been purchased by the Commission, however, because the Commission did not yet exist. Instead, each of the four political caucuses (Senate Republicans, Senate Democrats, House Republicans, and House Democrats) purchased its own computer system with caucus funds and guarded it jealously. By the time the Commission began its formal business in the summer of 1991, each political caucus thus possessed a well-trained staff of computer operators, custom-made software, and the ability to produce computerized maps in an endless array of sizes, geographic regions, and color-codings.

What happened once these maps were generated, however, was largely unobserved by the press or the public. The Pennsylvania Sunshine Act secures "the right of the public to be present at all meetings of agencies and to witness the deliberation, policy formulation and decision-making of agencies."[145] Citizens of the Commonwealth are thus entitled to receive notice and the opportunity to attend all meetings of agencies where any agency business is discussed or acted upon.[146] The Legislative Reapportionment Commission deemed itself to be an "agency" within the meaning of the Sunshine Act[147] and adopted an unwritten policy that all official actions and deliberations of a quorum of the five Commission members would be conducted in public, having given due notice through newspaper advertisements.[148] The only exception under the Sunshine Act related to "executive sessions" of the Commission, which were held directly prior to public meetings and which were related to specific confidential matters such as discussing potential litigation with counsel.[149]

As a practical matter, of course, it would be impossible for the Commission to conduct all of its day-to-day legwork — meetings with staff, for example — in public, or little would be accomplished. This is no less true of the legislature itself, which is constantly engaged in research, preparation, negotiation and preliminary work before stepping into the chambers of the House or Senate to deliberate, cast votes, and reach binding decisions. Consequently, a great deal of the work of the Commission was, and always had been, performed by staffs of each Commission member. Rough maps were prepared, tentative discussions were commenced; in reality, however, no final decision was ever made — and no deliberations of a quorum of the Commission members occurred — except in duly convened public meetings.

---

[145] 65 PA. CONS. STAT. ANN. §272(a) (Supp. 1993).

[146] *Id.* §272(b).

[147] *See* 65 PA. CONS. STAT. ANN. §273 (Supp. 1993).

[148] *See* 65 PA. CONS. STAT. ANN. §279 (Supp. 1993).

[149] 65 PA. CONS. STAT. ANN. §§277-78 (Supp. 1993).

In 1991, the process evolved fairly naturally. The Chairman, who had no independent access to map-making facilities, and no expertise with this computerized specialty, relied upon staffs from the four caucuses to produce "working maps" and proposals. Staff members would meet with the Chairman and Executive Director each week or two — in Pittsburgh or in Harrisburg — to discuss particular issues or specific regions of the state. Although in 1971 the Chairman had apparently met with Democrats and Republicans in separate blocks, Chairman Cindrich found it most productive to divide discussions into "House and Senate" issues, rather than "Democratic and Republican" issues. In practice, the House and Senate have much less in common than many citizens would expect; this was particularly true in reapportionment, where issues impacting on the House in creating 203 legislative districts differed widely from issues confronting the Senate in creating 50 districts.

Thus, the House Democratic and House Republican staffs, linked to their particular commission members, met with the Chairman and Executive Director on specified days; their Senate counterparts met on others. The principal negotiators for the caucuses were David Woods, Stephen MacNett and Mike Long (Senate Republicans); Mark McKillop and Michael Korposh (Senate Democrats); Stephen Dull (House Republicans); and Scott Casper (House Democrats). All of them were seasoned, talented political aides; most had worked on previous reapportionments. As the Chairman had indicated at the initial public meeting, the general approach he followed was to encourage cooperation and compromise among the "political" commissioners and their staffs. The Constitution, after all, had established them as members of this body because of their knowledge and expertise in political matters. Chairman Cindrich's primary role, at least initially, was to identify areas of disagreement and mediate disputes. At the same time, his role as a neutral citizen-participant was to carefully monitor the requirements of the federal and state constitutions — including equality of population, Federal Voting Rights Act, compactness, contiguity, and sanctity of political boundaries — and to ensure that these requirements were carefully safeguarded as the political process unfolded.

One benefit of this approach was that an inherent "checks and balances" system evolved in the negotiations between the political parties. To the extent that working maps unfairly impacted upon one party or another, or unnecessarily raised problems under the Constitution or statutes, one caucus or another (i.e. the party adversely affected) would inevitably raise the matter with the Chairman. The Chairman was then in a position to study the issue along with his own staff and to refuse to accept any proposal unless it resolved these shortcomings. The Chairman could (and did on many occasions) direct the caucus staffs to produce working maps which would reflect *his own* vision of a suitable solution. In this fashion, although not maintaining his own map-making facilities, the Chairman in effect initiated his own proposed maps relative to "problem" areas to ensure fairness and adherence to constitutional principles.

One difficulty which soon emerged related to acceptable "deviations" relating to population. The staffs of both the House and Senate were anxious to pin down a precise percentage that the Chairman would determine as "acceptable" in allowing variances from district to district. This flowed from the superemphasis on the one-person-one-vote issue that had dominated the two previous reapportionments. It also flowed from the fact that it was impossible for staffs to begin drawing maps without some type of outer boundaries regarding population deviation.

Otherwise, as one staffer explained, an entire map could turn into a "house of cards" if the Chairman later disapproved of the deviation in a single district.

By 1991, the case law as to the permissible range of population deviations was fairly well established. In *Brown v. Thomson*[150] in 1983, the United States Supreme Court had suggested that a *prima facie* case of discrimination was presumptively established where an apportionment plan contained a maximum population deviation of greater than 10%. In *Gaffney v. Cummings*[151] the Court had sustained a plan that allowed a 7.83% deviation in population. Furthermore, in *White v. Regester*,[152] the Court permitted a 9.9% deviation. Although in certain cases involving state (as opposed to congressional) reapportionment plans, even greater deviations were permitted,[153] particularly to preserve local political boundaries, the trend among federal courts was to insist on deviations much tighter than 10%, particularly given computer technology that permitted greater mathematical precision.[154]

Chairman Cindrich was reluctant to establish any hard-and-fast numbers. This was especially true after reviewing potential issues under the Voting Rights Act, as well as the provision of the Pennsylvania Constitution prohibiting splits of political subdivisions "unless absolutely necessary."[155] It became evident that the degree of flexibility permitted in population deviations might have to be directly adjusted depending upon the urgency of other constitutional and statutory mandates. In the end, the staffs adopted their own informal, internal guideline of a 5% deviation in the House and a 2% deviation in the Senate. Those numbers, however, were constantly subject to change. Indeed, later discussions concerning the resolution of Voting Rights Act issues included serious consideration of plans that included substantially higher deviations.

In sum, the staffs found it difficult to begin work without concrete guidelines as to deviation. The Chairman found it difficult to commit to hard-and-fast percentages when so many other factors would inevitably influence a final figure. In the end, the internal rules of thumb established by the staffs were not unreasonable; indeed, the final reapportionment plan slightly improved upon these goals. Future Commissions should continue to be wary of latching onto rigid, artificial percentages at the early stages of reapportionment. Concerns generated by the Voting Rights Act, the Pennsylvania Constitution's unique provisions, as well as other statutory and constitutional mandates, may continue to warrant creativity and flexibility on this matter as future reapportionments follow their own courses.

A final novel issue confronted by the 1991 Commission involved the access of citizens to the process. Because the individual political caucuses owned all of the available map-making facilities, it was impossible to provide working maps and computer programs to citizens wishing to participate. Such materials thus constituted the work product of individual commission members and their caucuses, rather than work-product of the Commission as a body. It would be no more appropriate to release such information to the public than it would be to release working notes and internal memoranda of legislators or their staffs.

---

[150] 462 U.S. 835 (1983).

[151] 412 U.S. 735 (1973).

[152] 412 U.S. 755 (1973).

[153] *See, e.g.*, Mahan v. Howell, 410 U.S. 315 (1973) (16.4% deviation).

[154] *See, e.g.*, Hastert v. State Bd. of Elections, 777 F. Supp. 634, 643 (N.D. Ill. 1991) (Selecting a congressional redistricting plan with total deviations of 0.00017% over a plan with 0.00297% and observing that "[t]he use of increasingly sophisticated computers in the congressional map drawing process has reduced population deviations to nearly infinitesimal proportions ....").

[155] *See* PA. CONST. art. II, §16.

At the same time, without access to the rapidly growing body of computer-generated information, the public's right to participate in the reapportionment process would become meaningless if certain raw materials were not available. Consequently, the Commission determined to make public all of the raw data and reports made available to the Commission itself.[156] Census data provided by the Bureau of Census, as well as racial data, were made available on computer disk. Other data made accessible included public comments to the proposed plans offered by citizens and groups, as well as the plans themselves and transcripts of the public meetings and hearings. Most of these raw materials were provided at a modest charge, to cover costs. The Commission specifically resolved, however, that working maps, computer software reflecting the internal processes of LDPC in compiling data, and other such materials would not be made available to the public.[157] These were in the nature of the Commission's work product and would have to be protected if any meaningful work were to be accomplished.

As the process developed, it became evident that a growing number of citizens wished to have access to population and racial data early on in the process, so that they could generate computerized maps of their own. Certain states, and New York City, had already begun making computer terminals and/or software directly available to interested citizens to further aid their participation. Although Pennsylvania was in no position to make these resources available in 1991, the Commission discussed this issue at executive session with legal counsel and agreed that the issue of public participation should be more fully explored (with an eye towards greater citizen participation) before the 2001 Commission commenced its work.

---

[156] Transcript of the Legislative Reapportionment Commission Meeting 8-10 (July 17, 1991) (Resolution #2F) (State Archives).
[157] *Id.*

VI.
PUBLIC HEARINGS AND PRELIMINARY PLAN

A. Initial Hearings

The 1991 Commission determined that receiving public input before drafting a preliminary plan was as essential as soliciting public comment after a tentative plan was on paper. Thus, the Commission publicized and scheduled a full day of public hearings on September 5, 1991, in the Capitol, to address "issues of state-wide importance in the reapportionment of Pennsylvania."[158]

For purposes of administrative efficiency and to avoid disjointed discussion of a plethora of localized issues, the Commission exercised some degree of control over the subject matter of the public hearing. Potential speakers were required to submit a brief summary of their proposed remarks to the Executive Director in advance and suitable topics were approved based upon their relevance to "issues of statewide concern." Purely local issues — for example, contentions that a boundary in a particular municipality should remain undisturbed — were generally dealt with by inviting the citizen to submit his or her comments in writing to the Commission for circulation, rather than through an oral presentation. This was consistent with the Commission's earlier conclusion that meetings, although open to the public, should not be participatory except to the extent that the Commission deemed such participation fruitful.[159] Not only did this approach avoid the problems of "free-for-alls" breaking out, but it also was essential if the Commission was to meet its internal deadline of September 16th to draft a preliminary plan[160] and its actual deadline of September 25th based upon counsel's calculation of the 90-day time period.[161]

The Commission's public hearing of September 5, 1991, was a watershed in many ways. For the first time in the history of the reapportionment process in Pennsylvania, racial issues, rather than one-person-one-vote concerns, dominated the discussion by citizens and legislators alike. The Federal Voting Rights Act, as amended in 1982, became the focal point for the Commission's concerns and opened up wide new vistas of debate in reapportioning Pennsylvania according to federal law.

Speakers at the public hearing included representatives from the NAACP, the Philadelphia Latino Voting Rights Act Committee, the Pennsylvania Farmers Union, the League of Women Voters, Blacks Networking for Progress, the Barristers Association of Philadelphia, the Republican State Committee, various unaffiliated citizens, and state legislators.[162] Although a host of important concerns were raised, several speakers' testimony became particularly relevant as the reapportionment process unfolded.

Barton Fields, of the Harrisburg office of the NAACP, submitted testimony prepared by the NAACP's National Redistricting Project in Baltimore, Maryland. The NAACP took the strong position that, in light of amendments to the Voting Rights Act promulgated by Congress in 1982, the Commission was obligated to

---

[158] *See* Minutes of Public Meeting (Sept. 5, 1991) (State Archives).

[159] *See* Transcript of the Legislative Reapportionment Commission Meeting 51-53 (July 17, 1991) (State Archives).

[160] *Id.* at 51; Resolution #2K.

[161] *Id.* at 48.

[162] *See* Minutes of Public Meeting (Sept. 5, 1991); Transcript of Public Hearing of the Legislative Reapportionment Commission (Sept. 5, 1991) (State Archives).

create "majority-minority" districts wherever it could. "[A]ny action that results in the dilution of the black community's voting strength," stated the NAACP spokesman, "is a violation of the Act."[163] An absence of discriminatory intent was no longer relevant under the Voting Rights Act, the NAACP pointed out. If the Commission could create minority districts but did not create them, it was violating federal law. Moreover, a district with a bare majority of 50% African-Americans was not sufficient to satisfy the Voting Rights Act under the recent case law. Rather, the racial minority had to be given an "equitable chance to elect candidates of choice," requiring generally a 65% super-majority if blacks were to be given a realistic chance to make their votes count.[164]

Professor Abigail Thernstrom, an adjunct professor of political science at Boston University, with a Ph.D. from Harvard University, testified vigorously to the contrary.[165] Dr. Thernstrom was the author of a controversial book published by Harvard University Press in 1987, entitled *Whose Votes Count?: Affirmative Action and Minority Voting Rights.*[166] The premise of Professor Thernstrom's award-winning book, as well as her testimony, was that the Voting Rights Act was not designed to institute "de facto apartheid."[167] Dr. Thernstrom argued that the 1982 Amendments to the Voting Rights Act were not fashioned to mandate that reapportionment bodies draw the maximum number of "safe" minority districts or engage in affirmative "racial gerrymandering." Nor did the recent Supreme Court case in *Thornburg v. Gingles*[168] require such a course. According to Dr. Thernstrom, the racial gerrymandering approach adopted by so many states after *Gingles* was based upon a faulty assumption that "whites can't represent blacks and blacks can't represent whites."[169] It would cause society to "walk backwards on the race relations front towards a more racially divided society," she testified, and lead to black isolation if the Pennsylvania Commission were to follow this blind path.[170] In the end, Dr. Thernstrom contended, black citizens would be left with less representation, rather than more, "since the number of white candidates and legislators who need black support to win will have been reduced by the racial gerrymandering."[171] Dr. Thernstrom urged that states like Pennsylvania should not "cave in" to what she deemed a "cynical alliance between Republicans and civil rights groups on voting rights matters," because such racial gerrymandering would ultimately lead to a negative impact on black citizens throughout the Commonwealth.[172]

Patricia DeCarlo, Co-chair of the Philadelphia Latino Voting Rights Committee, fundamentally disagreed with Dr. Thernstrom. She insisted that the Latino community in Philadelphia was entitled to affirmative action by the Commission to create districts in which Latino citizens could elect candidates of choice.[173] Ms. DeCarlo noted that it was only through aggressive efforts in the 1981 reapportion-

---

[163] Transcript of Public Hearings 10 (Sept. 5, 1991) (State Archives).
[164] *Id.* at 13-14.
[165] *Id.* at 17-49.
[166] *See* ABIGAIL THERNSTROM, WHOSE VOTES COUNT?: AFFIRMATIVE ACTION AND MINORITY VOTING RIGHTS (1987).
[167] Transcript of Public Hearings 18 (Sept. 5, 1991) (State Archives).
[168] 478 U.S. 30 (1986).
[169] Transcript of Public Hearings 22 (Sept. 5, 1991) (State Archives).
[170] *Id.* at 24.
[171] *Id.*
[172] *Id.* at 32-33, 49.
[173] *Id.* at 50-61.

ment process that a single legislative district in Philadelphia (the 180th) had been created with sufficient Latino population to elect Representative Ralph Acosta, a Latino. In 1991, she argued, the Latino community in Philadelphia was sufficiently large and geographically compact to allow the creation of one legislative district (180th) in which Latinos constituted a majority of over 60%; one legislative district (179th) in which a significant Latino influence (of over 30%) would be present; and one senatorial district in the northeast area of Philadelphia which encompassed most of the Latino population and the growth area of the Latino community.[174] Ms. DeCarlo concluded by noting that the socioeconomic indicators of the Latino community were the worst of any racial minority in Philadelphia: 38% unemployment and a 73% high school drop-out rate.[175] Thus, voting empowerment by the Commission was essential.

Blaine A. Brown, Deputy Chairman of the Republican State Committee, echoed the views of the NAACP and the Philadelphia Latino Voting Rights Committee. Drawing "majority-minority" and "minority influenced" districts, he contended, should be viewed as a mandate of the Commission.[176] Moreover, Mr. Brown urged that population losses in Philadelphia and Allegheny County dictated that those areas should lose seats. At the same time, areas of population growth in the suburbs, particularly the southeast, should gain seats.[177]

Speakers also stepped forward on issues unrelated to minority voting rights. A spokeswoman for the League of Women Voters, Marilyn Manchester, advised the Commission to be particularly wary of splits of boroughs, townships or cities "unless absolutely necessary." Such splits, she stated, had an adverse impact upon the integrity of neighborhoods and communities of interest.[178] Similarly, Joseph Gambescia, a citizen of Delaware County residing in the 166th legislative district, warned that the destruction of municipal boundaries in legislative map-making would produce an adverse impact upon school districts. The strength of any such public unit, he contended, was diluted if it was split between more than one legislator, thus depriving it of a unified voice in the State Capitol.[179]

Having considered the testimony of these and other individuals in oral and written form, the Commission adjourned and began work in earnest on a preliminary reapportionment plan.

As part of its fact-gathering process, the Commission, for the first time in that body's history, travelled to Philadelphia to meet with representatives of affected minority groups. This tour of minority communities in Philadelphia took place on September 11, 1991, and proved to be extremely beneficial in several ways. In part, the trip was prompted by the fact that both the Chairman and Executive Director were lifelong residents of Pittsburgh and had little first-hand sense of the Latino and African-American communities on the other end of the state. The trip was also prompted by the desire of all Commission members and the Chief Counsel to get a clear picture of minority issues and community concerns in the state's largest city, particularly since the Federal Voting Rights Act was looming as a dominant factor in the reapportionment work of 1991.

---

[174] Id. at 52-53.
[175] Id. at 54.
[176] Id. at 97-125.
[177] Id. at 101-04.
[178] Id. at 65-69.
[179] Id. at 71-80.

The Commission met with various minority groups in Philadelphia including the Philadelphia Latino Voting Rights Committee (meeting at *Central Pedro Claver*) and the Philadelphia Chapter of the NAACP (meeting at the Urban Education Center). The benefit of this physical tour of Philadelphia and its neighborhoods was that a diverse group of Commission members and their staffs were able to obtain a first-hand picture of minority communities in the single square of Pennsylvania where most voting rights issues would inevitably have to be fought out.

B. Vote on the Preliminary Plan

On September 23, 1991, the Commission convened to vote on a preliminary reapportionment plan.[180] This date fell one week after the Commission's own internal deadline of September 16th to draft a preliminary plan and two days before the actual constitutional deadline. The Chairman announced that the Commission members and their staffs had worked through the night without sleep and were still unable to produce a preliminary plan in a form satisfactory for a vote. Chairman Cindrich noted that the significant shift in population within Pennsylvania, from west to east and southeast, had created a difficult task since it was inevitable that a number of incumbent legislators would lose their seats. This situation led to a temporary political gridlock. Despite two recesses, the Commission was unable to put a plan on the table with adequate legal descriptions. Therefore, over the objections of Senator Loeper, the Commission meeting was recessed until September 25th, the actual constitutional deadline.[181]

Two days later, the Commission reconvened in the State Capitol, with a preliminary reapportionment plan now on the table for a vote.[182] Representative Kukovich moved that the Commission approve plans marked Senate No. 1 and House No. 1 (later substituted with No. 1-A), as generated by the Legislative Data Processing Center at the request of the Commission Chairman. Senator Loeper objected to Senate No. 1, primarily because it merged a Republican and Democratic seat in the Pittsburgh area to deal with population loss, rather than merging two Democratic seats in the specific districts where the greatest population losses had taken place.[183] Senator Loeper further objected to the merger because it cut off an existing incumbent's term (that of Senator Pecora) after two years.[184] Senator Loeper offered various amendments to the proposed preliminary plan which would have preserved the incumbency of Senator Pecora in the 44th District in western Pennsylvania, merged the districts where greater population losses had occurred, and increased the minority population in one district. All of these proposals failed.[185]

After further debate, the Commission voted unanimously to adopt the proposed preliminary plan of reapportionment for the House (House No. 1-A). As to the Senate plan, the Commission voted 4-1 to approve the original proposal, with Senator Loeper opposing the preliminary plan for the reasons previously stated.[186] The Chairman thereafter directed the Executive Director to file the preliminary plan with the Secretary of the Commonwealth before the end of the constitutional

---

[180] Transcript of Legislative Reapportionment Commission Hearing (Sept. 23, 1991) (State Archives).
[181] *Id.* at 8-14.
[182] Transcript of Legislative Reapportionment Commission Hearing (Sept. 25, 1991) (State Archives).
[183] *Id.* at 9-12.
[184] *Id.* at 12-13.
[185] *Id.* at 16-44.
[186] *Id.* at 69-72.

deadline (that same day), and scheduled a public hearing on October 9, 1991, for the purpose of considering public comment to the preliminary plan. Citizens interested in providing testimony were requested to submit a written summary of their proposed comments to the Executive Director no later than October 7, 1991, so that the meeting could be properly structured and controlled.[187]

The Preliminary Reapportionment Plan filed with the Secretary of the Commonwealth contained lengthy legal descriptions, as required by the Constitution, along with maps. The Secretary immediately began the tedious process of preparing this data for publication in newspapers throughout the Commonwealth; the Secretary completed this task with a barrage of newspaper advertisements during the week of October 6, 1991. The actual 30-day comment period established by the Constitution would expire on October 25, 1991, at midnight.[188]

C. Second Hearings — Response to the Preliminary Plan

On October 9, 1991, the Commission again assembled in the State Capitol to hear testimony from affected citizens and groups regarding the preliminary plan of reapportionment.[189] The Commission had been inundated with petitions, fax messages, written objections, and requests to provide testimony. From these, duplicative and tangential matters were eliminated from the pool of responses. Thirty individuals and groups were invited to provide oral testimony at the hearing, many of whom centered their comments around a handful of core issues.

One cluster of vigorous debate and comment pertained to the elimination of the 44th Senatorial District outside Pittsburgh, designed to deal with population shifts towards the east. Directly affected by this aspect of the preliminary plan was Senator Frank Pecora (R., Penn Hills), who appeared with busloads of supporters and constituents to protest the proposed redistricting. Attorney Anthony Martin, counsel for Pecora, took the floor and suggested that nothing in the Constitution permitted the Commission to terminate this incumbent legislator's term in midstream. Moreover, he contended, the action of the Commission stripped the voters of the 44th District of their right to be represented by the senator whom they had elected for a four-year term. Further, he asserted that these voters were essentially being disenfranchised. Attorney Martin proposed a revised plan by which 130,000 citizens from each of the odd-numbered senatorial districts in western Pennsylvania (37th, 43rd, 45th) would be moved into adjoining even-numbered districts, thus collapsing the three odd districts into two, and creating new districts with a population deviation of approximately 10%.[190]

Even more controversial was the testimony of Charles Kindle, a constituent of Senator Pecora and President of the Penn Hills Chapter of the NAACP.[191] Mr. Kindle submitted a proposal which would create a minority district comprised of 51% African-Americans in Allegheny County, leaving the existing 44th District largely intact. Under questioning from the Commission, Mr. Kindle acknowledged that his plan, which split numerous municipal boundaries including Penn Hills,

---

[187] *Id.* at 72-73.
[188] *Id.* at 73.
[189] Transcript of Legislative Reapportionment Commission Meeting (Oct. 9, 1991) (State Archives).
[190] *Id.* at 13-24. Citizen Dan Torisky, a constituent in the existing Pecora District, echoed this sentiment and stated that although he was a Democrat, he had "voted for Senator Pecora in the last election expecting him to represent us in Harrisburg for four years." *Id.* at 27.
[191] *Id.* at 37-54.

was not sanctioned by the national or state offices of the NAACP.[192] He also acknowledged that the data and printout were provided to him by Senator Pecora.[193] Next, a heated exchange erupted between Kindle, Senator Mellow, and Chairman Cindrich, in which Kindle and Senator Pecora charged the Commission with racism. Following this exchange, Senator Pecora and a large number of citizens marched out of the meeting, having concluded their testimony.[194]

Patricia DeCarlo, Co-chair of the Philadelphia Latino Voting Rights Committee, next challenged the impact of the preliminary plan on the Latino community in Philadelphia.[195] In response to the Chairman's introductory remarks regarding the beneficial nature of his tour of the Latino neighborhoods in Philadelphia, Ms. DeCarlo replied: "I am afraid that perhaps we did not do as good a job of giving you a tour of the community if your proposed plan is a reflection of that tour."[196]

Ms. DeCarlo declared that the proposed 179th Legislative District was a "disaster," decreasing the Latino population from the proposed 34% to 23%, despite a significant increase in the Latino population in that district. She asserted that the district was intentionally drawn in an "absurd" configuration to eliminate a Latino challenger to incumbent Representative Rieger.[197] It also moved Latinos into the "dangerous" area of Fishtown — "you cross Front Street and you take life into your hands, and I'm serious about that" — rather than grouping these citizens in areas of growth in the north and east.[198] Although the 180th Legislative District contained a satisfactory percentage of the Latino population (63%), it accomplished this result by emasculating certain areas of the Latino community, including a drug rehabilitation center split between two districts.[199] As to the senate, she charged, the proposed districts allowed Latinos "no chance of influencing the election of the state Senator in that area," whereas the Latino proposal would have created a Senate district with a 28% Latino population.[200]

Samuel L. Walters, Assistant General Counsel of the national office of the NAACP handling the national redistricting project, likewise blasted the preliminary plan.[201] He first expressed dismay that the NAACP had experienced delays in obtaining racial breakdown data and had not yet obtained "voting age population" data from the Commission. This information, he stated, was essential to performing meaningful analysis under the Voting Rights Act and was routinely supplied by many states simultaneously with the plan itself.[202]

More significantly, Attorney Walters provided his own rough sketches of data to demonstrate that fifteen "majority-minority" House districts could be created in Philadelphia, in contrast to the thirteen minority districts created by the Com-

---

[192] *Id.* at 47-48.
[193] *Id.* at 51-53.
[194] *Id.* at 58-59.
[195] *Id.* at 92-106.
[196] *Id.* at 93.
[197] *Id.* at 93-94.
[198] *Id.* at 95-96.
[199] *Id.* at 98, 101-02.
[200] *Id.* at 99.
[201] *Id.* at 160-78.
[202] *Id.* at 161-63. It was later clarified that the NAACP had requested only the preliminary plan itself, which (according to Article II, Section 17 of the Pennsylvania Constitution), relates to population data and not to racial data. *Id.* at 177-178. In any event, the requested data was immediately provided. Indeed, racial data had been provided free of charge, on computer disk, to all who requested it. *Id.* at 4-5.

mission in the preliminary plan.[203] Likewise, four majority-minority seats could be created in the Senate in Philadelphia, through several different configurations,[204] in contrast to the three created by the Commission. Although Attorney Walters stressed that the NAACP did not intend to actually draw boundary lines because they had no concrete information as to the political and community contours of Philadelphia, Attorney Walters established a benchmark to show that markedly better results could be achieved under the Voting Rights Act.[205]

Finally, in response to questioning from Chief Counsel Harmelin, Attorney Walters indicated that the recent decision of a three-judge federal district court panel in Ohio, in *Armour v. Ohio*,[206] required the creation of "minority influenced" districts in areas like Dauphin County and Allegheny County, particularly where percentages totalling 50% minorities could be achieved.[207]

On a related front, citizens from Cheltenham and Lower Moreland Townships, outside of the city of Philadelphia, appeared *en masse* to oppose being included in the predominantly Philadelphia-driven senatorial districts. Senator Stewart Greenleaf presented petitions from over 2,000 citizens objecting to the "annexation" of those Montgomery County areas into the 4th and 5th Senatorial District in Philadelphia. "I have deep concerns," stated Senator Greenleaf, "that it will be next to impossible to represent two regions with as much divergence and interests and needs as Philadelphia and these suburban communities."[208]

Bernard Borine, a Commissioner of Cheltenham Township, presented 3,000 additional signatures on petitions and charged that "[t]he minor surgery needed to reach the magic number [in population] could have been performed with a scalpel. Instead it was done with a chain saw."[209] He further asserted that such a merger would lead to serious problems for both Montgomery County communities, because any senator would inevitably favor the city in funding issues, to the serious detriment of the suburbs.

Chairman Cindrich responded to these assertions by noting that extending senatorial districts outside of the city of Philadelphia was necessary in light of the one-person-one-vote principle. In the city itself, there were approximately 160,000 more citizens than would fit into six districts, yet approximately 237,000 citizens were required to create a seventh district.[210] As the Chairman had explained earlier in the hearings, "if you were looking down at Pennsylvania and you had a great big huge cookie cutter, you would be creating districts and trying to get 237,000 people in each district. When you start to do that at any given point in the state, you run out of people pretty soon .... It's people we're concerned with, not voting districts."[211] In response to the Chairman's question as to where the citizens would come from to complete a seventh district based upon 160,000 excess citizens in Philadelphia, Senator Greenleaf's reply was that they should come from Lower Bucks County. The Chairman's retort was that this would spark the same objec-

---

[203] *Id.* at 164-65.

[204] *Id.* at 168-69.

[205] *Id.* at 165-66.

[206] 775 F. Supp. 1044 (N.D. Ohio 1991).

[207] Transcript of Legislative Reapportionment Commission Meeting 174-76 (Oct. 9, 1991) (State Archives).

[208] *Id.* at 111.

[209] *Id.* at 112.

[210] *Id.* at 117-19.

[211] *Id.* at 59-60.

tions lodged by Cheltenham and Lower Moreland; it would simply move the geography of the complainants.[212]

Attorney Richard Glanton, of the Republican City Committee of Philadelphia, presented testimony similar to that of NAACP Attorney Samuel Walters. Attorney Glanton contended that four majority-minority senatorial seats could be created in Philadelphia.[213] Under questioning by Senator Mellow, it was determined that the city of Philadelphia contained an African-American population of approximately 38%, and an additional Latino and Asian population of 4%, for a total minority population of 42% of the city. At the same time, Senator Mellow pointed out that the city of Philadelphia already encompassed three majority-minority seats in the Senate, or 43% of the total senatorial seats in that city. Thus, argued Senator Mellow, creation of a fourth minority seat in effect would result in an overrepresentation of minorities.[214]

A string of speakers next presented testimony regarding unnecessary "splits" of political subdivisions, as well as noncompact districts being drawn for political purposes. Citizen Lawrence Roberts, of the 51st Legislative District near Uniontown, asserted that the previously compact and contiguous district in which he lived had been transformed into a "funny looking creature," largely to protect Representative Fred Taylor against whom he had run in 1990 and nearly unseated.[215] Roberts charged, in essence, that he had been intentionally gerrymandered out of the district.[216] Objections were also lodged by disgruntled citizens of the 118th Legislative District in Luzerne and Lackawanna Counties,[217] the 68th Legislative District in Tioga and Potter Counties,[218] the 74th Legislative District in Curwensville and Pike Township,[219] and the 199th Legislative District in York County,[220] among others.

Following the presentation of testimony from thirty speakers, the Commission adjourned. All remaining public comments would have to be presented to the Commission by midnight, October 25th, via mail. At that time the thirty-day public comment period established by the Commission would expire.

In the brisk month of business that followed, the Executive Director reviewed thousands of letters, written comments, petitions, telephone messages, and other responses from citizens. These were summarized in written form, according to broad categories. Summaries were then circulated to each Commission member and staff. Prior to taking action on a Final Plan, the Commission members attempted to consider all of the thousands of complaints and comments in a systematic fashion. Never before had such a massive amount of public comment been received by this body and never before had the Commission faced the prospect of making such significant changes in a preliminary plan prior to voting on a final plan of reapportionment.

---

[212] *Id.* at 118-22.
[213] *Id.* at 141-47, 153-60.
[214] *Id.* at 158-60.
[215] *Id.* at 74-80.
[216] *Id.* at 79-80.
[217] *Id.* at 178-85.
[218] *Id.* at 186-90.
[219] *Id.* at 190-91.
[220] *Id.* at 193-97.

VII.
NEW LEGAL FRONTIERS FACE
THE COMMISSION (THE VOTING RIGHTS ACT)

A. History: Fifteenth Amendment to *Thornburg v. Gingles*

New legal issues, dominated by the Federal Voting Rights Act, would soon drive the reapportionment process towards a fiery conclusion. The Voting Rights Act was a piece of civil rights legislation adopted under the Presidency of Lyndon B. Johnson, shortly after the assassination of President John F. Kennedy.[221] This law was designed to remedy a century of blatant and covert practices by states that had skillfully denied African-Americans and other minorities of a meaningful opportunity to vote, particularly, although not exclusively, in the South.

The Fifteenth Amendment to the United States Constitution, ratified in 1870, had guaranteed that "[t]he right of citizens of the United States to vote shall not be denied or abridged by the United States or by any State on account of race, color, or previous condition of servitude."[222] In the ninety-five years following the adoption of the Fifteenth Amendment, however, state and local governments found a host of creative ways to circumvent the intent of the provision, including literacy tests, poll taxes, and other not-so-subtle methods of excluding African-Americans and other minorities from the voting booths. Congress therefore designed the Voting Rights Act of 1965 to confront these abuses head-on, primarily by placing the burden on states with a history of questionable practices to justify those practices or have them dismantled.

One of the most significant corridors in which the Voting Rights Act had become relevant, of course, was the area of reapportionment. Section 5 of the Voting Rights Act required certain state and local governments "covered" by the Act to obtain "preclearance" with the U.S. Department of Justice or the U.S. District Court for the District of Columbia before any changes in voting standards, practices, or procedures could be made.[223] At first, the preclearance requirements were placed on only the few jurisdictions that maintained literacy tests and other forms of blatant discrimination in voting qualifications as of the presidential election of 1964.[224] However, subsequent amendments in 1970, 1975, and 1982 broadened the reach of the Voting Rights Act; consequently 22 states or parts of states were now covered by the Section 5 preclearance requirements.[225] This meant, for one thing, that these jurisdictions were required to preclear their reapportionment plans with the U.S. Department of Justice or the federal courts, placing an immediate check upon the ability of states to establish continued barriers to equality in voting rights.[226] It also meant that any state or covered jurisdiction which failed to preclear its reapportionment plan or other electoral changes with the U.S. Depart-

---

[221] Pub. L. No. 89-110, Title I, Aug. 6, 1965. The Voting Rights Act is now codified at 42 U.S.C. §§1791 *et seq.* (1982).

[222] U.S. CONST. amend. XV, §1.

[223] *See* 42 U.S.C. §1973c (1982).

[224] *Id.*

[225] *See* National Conference of State Legislatures, REAPPORTIONMENT LAW: THE 1990's, at 42-4 (1989).

[226] The regulations governing the preclearance process are found in the Procedures for the Administration of Section 5 of the Voting Rights Act of 1965. 28 C.F.R. §51 (1988).

ment of Justice, or ignored the Department's objections to the plan, might immediately face a lawsuit in federal court before a three-judge panel.[227]

Pennsylvania, because it lacked a history of overt discrimination in voting practices, was not included in the lineup of preclearance states. Nonetheless, Pennsylvania fell under the broader ambit of Section 2 of the Act, which prohibited any state or political subdivision from imposing any voting qualification, standard, practice, or procedure that resulted in denial or abridgement of any United States citizen's right to vote on account of race, color, or status as a member of a minority group.[228]

Perhaps the most significant in a series of amendments to the Voting Rights Act had occurred in 1982, when Congress altered the Act in response to the decision of the U.S. Supreme Court in *City of Mobile v. Bolden*.[229] In *Bolden*, the Court had diverged from a string of earlier cases and held that plaintiffs were required to prove an *intent* to discriminate to establish a violation of the Fifteenth Amendment and to make out a vote dilution claim under the Voting Rights Act. This "intent" test placed a heavy burden on plaintiffs, making it virtually impossible to prove a violation of the Act without a smoking gun, i.e. proof of intent by the state legislature to discriminate. Congress disapproved of this stringent interpretation of the Voting Rights Act and, in 1982, amended the Act to embody a more workable "results" test which the Court had advanced in earlier cases.[230] The resulting language of the Voting Rights Act, following the 1982 Amendments, provided in relevant part:

> (a) No voting qualification or prerequisite to voting or standard, practice, or procedure shall be imposed or applied by any state or political subdivision in a manner which results in a denial or abridgement of the right of any citizen of the United States to vote on account of race or color ....

> (b) A violation of subsection (a) of this section is established if, based on the totality of circumstances, it is shown that the political processes leading to nomination or election in the state or political subdivision are not equally open to participation by members of a class of citizens protected by subsection (a) of this section in that its members have less opportunity than other members of the electorate to participate in the political process and to elect representatives of their choice. The extent to which members of a protected class have been elected to office in the state or political subdivision is one circumstance which may be considered: Provided, that nothing in this section establishes a right to have members of a protected class elected in numbers equal to their proportion in the population.[231]

In this manner, the Voting Rights Act as amended in 1982 now provided a statutory cause of action for those asserting that a voting standard, practice or procedure "resulted" in discrimination based upon race.

---

[227] *See* 42 U.S.C. §1973c; 28 U.S.C. §2284(a) (1978).

[228] *See* Act of June 29, 1982, Pub. L. No. 97-205, §3, 96 Stat. 131, 134 (codified at 42 U.S.C. §1973a (1982)).

[229] 446 U.S. 55 (1980).

[230] *See, e.g.,* White v. Regester, 412 U.S. 755 (1973); Whitcomb v. Chavis, 403 U.S. 124 (1971); Zimmer v. McKeithen, 485 F.2d 1297 (5th Cir. 1973), *aff'd per curiam on other grounds sub nom.* East Carroll Parish Sch. Bd. v. Marshall, 424 U.S. 636 (1976).

[231] 42 U.S.C. §1973 (1982).

The first major decision of the Supreme Court interpreting the 1982 amendments, *Thornburg v. Gingles*,[232] proved to have a dramatic impact upon the 1991 reapportionment process in Pennsylvania, as it did throughout the rest of the nation. In *Gingles*, plaintiffs had challenged the use of multimember state house districts, as well as several state senate districts, under a North Carolina redistricting plan. The plan had been "precleared" under Section 5 of the Voting Rights Act by the U.S. Department of Justice.

The Supreme Court reviewed the legislative history of Section 2 of the Act to determine whether the North Carolina plan met the "results" test of the amended Voting Rights Act. The Court observed that the essence of a Section 2 claim was that some electoral law, practice, or structure "interacts with social and historical conditions to cause an inequality in the opportunities enjoyed by black and white voters to elect their preferred representatives."[233] In light of the 1982 amendments, the question turned on whether "'as a result of the challenged practice or structure plaintiffs do not have an equal opportunity to participate in the political processes and to elect candidates of their choice.'"[234] Writing for the majority, Justice Brennan concluded that all but one of the challenged multimember districts created by the North Carolina legislature violated the Voting Rights Act.

Significantly, the *Gingles* opinion established a fairly concrete test for determining whether legislative districts violated the newly-amended Act. Under *Gingles*, the Supreme Court required minority plaintiffs to prove three elements to show that a plan impaired their opportunity to elect candidates of choice. The minority plaintiffs would be required to show that:

1. The minority group was sufficiently large and geographically compact to constitute a majority in a single-member district.

2. The minority group was politically cohesive.

3. In the absence of special circumstances, "bloc voting" by the white majority usually defeated the minority's candidate of choice.[235]

The *Gingles* Court further noted that certain specific factors, derived from the Senate report relating to the 1982 Amendments, had to be examined to determine if a Section 2 claim had been made out by minority plaintiffs. These factors included:

1. The history of voting-related discrimination in the state or political subdivision;

2. The extent to which voting in the elections of the state or political subdivision is racially polarized;

3. The extent to which the state or political subdivision has used voting practices or procedures that tend to enhance the opportunity for discrimination against the minority group, such as unusually large election districts, majority vote requirements, and prohibitions against bullet voting;

---

[232] 478 U.S. 30 (1986).

[233] 478 U.S. at 47.

[234] *Id.* at 44 (citing S. REP. NO. 417, 97th Cong., 2d Sess. 28 (1982), *reprinted in* 1982 U.S.C.C.A.N. 177, 206).

[235] *Id.* at 49-51.

4. The exclusion of members of the minority group from candidate slating processes;

5. The extent to which minority group members bear the effects of past discrimination in areas such as education, employment, and health, which hinder their ability to participate effectively in the political process;

6. The use of overt or subtle racial appeals in political campaigns, and;

7. The extent to which members of the minority group have been elected to public office in the jurisdiction.[236]

In the context of the multi-member districts at issue in *Gingles*, the Court noted that the second and seventh factors were the most important to the plaintiffs' Section 2 claim.[237] The Court also stated that these factors "are supportive of, but *not essential to*," a minority voter's Section 2 claims.[238]

Although the *Gingles* majority acknowledged that the Senate report espoused a "flexible, fact-intensive" test for Section 2 violations, the Court also limited the circumstances under which plaintiffs could prove a Section 2 violation. First, electoral devices such as at-large elections would not be considered *per se* violations of Section 2. Second, at-large elections and the lack of proportional representation alone would not establish a violation of Section 2. Third, the "results" test would not assume the existence of racial bloc voting; rather, plaintiffs would be required to prove it.[239]

The *Gingles* decision arguably required reapportionment bodies to seek out and create majority-minority districts to allow minority voters to elect candidates of their choice. For example, the Supreme Court had made clear in 1991 that the Voting Rights Act could be used to invalidate discriminatory reapportionment plans.[240] Other recent lower court decisions seemed to interpret *Gingles* to stand for the proposition that if a majority-minority district *could* be created, it *had to be* created.[241] Thus, the Pennsylvania Legislative Reapportionment Commission, like similar bodies in other states, was hurled into new terrain that seemed to require active "racial gerrymandering" in order to achieve federally mandated goals. Armed with the newly articulated *Gingles* standards that had already generated considerable public controversy in its own hearings in Harrisburg, the Commission moved forward to assess the ramifications of *Gingles* in dealing with the objections to the Preliminary Plan.

B. What Constitutes a Majority-Minority District?

The still-evolving *Gingles* standard left open a number of major issues that required the immediate attention of the Commission if a legally defensible reapportionment plan was to be fashioned. This was particularly true in light of the

---

[236] *Id.* at 44-45.

[237] *Id.* at 48-49 n. 15 (indicating that these factors must have different weights to further the congressional policies of Section 2).

[238] *Id.*

[239] *Id.* at 46.

[240] Chisom v. Roemer, 111 S. Ct. 2354 (1991).

[241] *See, e.g.,* Jeffers v. Clinton, 730 F. Supp. 196 (E.D. Ark. 1989), *aff'd,* 498 U.S. 1019 (1991); Garza v. County of Los Angeles, 756 F. Supp. 1298 (C.D. Cal. 1990), *aff'd in part, vacated in part,* 918 F.2d 763 (9th Cir. 1990), *cert. denied,* 498 U.S. 1028 (1991).

hearings held after the Preliminary Plan was filed. These hearings exposed serious concerns by the African-American and Latino communities, particularly in Philadelphia, which the Commission had to address directly and frankly.

The first of the question marks under the Voting Rights Act related to the definition of a majority-minority district. If *Gingles* in fact required the creation of majority African-American and Latino districts wherever they could be created (Dr. Abigail Thernstrom's testimony to the contrary), what minority percentage was sufficient to constitute a majority-minority district? In the *Gingles* district court opinion, the lower court had held that "no aggregation of less than 50% of an area's *voting age population* can possibly constitute an effective voting majority."[242] This finding was never challenged in the Supreme Court's decision and thus carried a whiff of authority. A number of other federal decisions had focussed on *voting age population* rather than *total minority population*,[243] again suggesting that this was the proper standard.

The significance of this issue for the Commission was dramatic. If *voting age population* rather than *total population* were the standard, this meant that *Gingles* required the Commission to in effect create supermajority districts containing *well over 50%* in raw minority population. This interpretation had a certain intellectual appeal. If the purpose of *Gingles* and the Voting Rights Act were to allow minority citizens to elect candidates of their choice, a district containing a flat 50% of raw population would probably not accomplish that goal. Not all citizens, minority or otherwise, are old enough to vote. Moreover, minority communities historically fall below the norm in the number of citizens registered to vote. Thus, the rule of thumb reported in much of the Voting Rights Act literature was that districts containing approximately 65% total minority population would represent the ideal in allowing minorities to elect candidates of choice.[244] Such a supermajority would allow a cushion to preserve a voting age population of well over 50%. It would also preserve some leeway based upon historically lower registration and lower voter turnout in minority communities. Thus, although no Supreme Court case had pronounced that the Voting Rights Act mandated a 65% supermajority to create effective majority-minority seats, the Commission remained acutely aware that a percentage of total minority population comfortably in excess of 50% would most likely be required and that any variation from the artificial 65% rule of thumb would most likely prompt careful scrutiny by the courts.

At the same time, the Commission understood that the creation of supermajority minority districts presented a double-edged sword. Although modern Voting Rights Act cases suggested that districts well over 50% total minority population were necessary to provide meaningful opportunities for African-Americans and

---

[242] *See* Gingles v. Edmisten, 590 F. Supp. 345, 381 n.3 (E.D.N.C. 1984) (emphasis added), *aff'd in part, rev'd in part sub nom.* Thornburg v. Gingles, 478 U.S. 30 (1986).

[243] *See, e.g.,* McNeil v. Springfield Park Dist., 851 F.2d 937, 944 (7th Cir. 1988), *cert. denied,* 490 U.S. 1031 (1989) (noting that only minorities of voting age can affect the potential to elect candidates of their choice); Jeffers v. Clinton, 730 F. Supp. at 199; Dillard v. Baldwin County Bd. of Educ., 686 F. Supp. 1459, 1469 (M.D. Ala. 1988); Romero v. City of Pomona, 665 F. Supp. 853, 857 (C.D. Cal. 1987), *aff'd,* 883 F.2d 1418 (9th Cir. 1989); Martin v. Allain, 658 F. Supp. 1183, 1198 (S.D. Miss. 1987). *Cf.* Garza v. County of Los Angeles, 918 F.2d at 774 (using total Latino population); League of Latin Am. Citizens v. Midland Indep. Sch. Dist., 658 F. Supp. 596, 606 (W.D. Tex. 1986), *aff'd,* 829 F.2d 546 (5th Cir. 1987) (same).

[244] *See, e.g.,* REAPPORTIONMENT LAW: THE 1990's, *supra* note 224, at 62; Ketchum v. Byrne, 740 F.2d 1398, 1415 (7th Cir. 1984), *cert. denied sub nom.* City Council of Chicago v. Ketchum, 471 U.S. 1135 (1985).

Latinos to elect candidates of choice, creating districts containing minorities in *overly high* percentages were just as illegitimate and illegal. "Packing" was a term that referred to the improper concentration of too many minority citizens into a single district, thereby "wasting" a percentage of minority votes and isolating minorities within a handful of over-stuffed districts.[245] Just as *Gingles* had provided no sharp guidelines as to the percentage of minority citizens necessary to create a legitimate majority-minority district, it provided no tangible guidepost as to what percentage might be too high. A handful of courts and a dusting of literature had suggested that any percentage exceeding 70% of total minority population could be viewed as "packing."[246] Thus, the Commission was required to walk a tightrope, particularly in Philadelphia, where a number of existing Senatorial and House districts exceeded 70% African-American population and were open to federal attack. To reshuffle the decks, however, might result in districts *less* than the 65% rule of thumb. Either way, the Commission faced a dangerous Hobson's choice.

C. The Question of "Minority Influenced" Districts

An equally perplexing issue in the wake of *Gingles* was whether the Commission was required to create so-called "minority influenced" districts that fell below a percentage sufficient to actually win an election. That is, where minority voters could not demonstrate that they would constitute a majority of voters in a particular district, but could still "influence" the outcome of an election, did Section 2 of the Voting Rights Act require the Commission to create such a district?

This question was sparked by Justice O'Connor's concurrence in *Gingles* (joined by Chief Justice Burger, and Justices Powell and Rehnquist). Justice O'Connor specifically left open the issue of "minority influenced" districts with the following comment:

> I express no view as to whether the ability of a minority group to constitute a majority in a single-member district should constitute a threshold requirement for a claim [under Section 2] .... I note, however, the artificiality of the Court's distinction between claims that a minority group's "ability *to elect* the representatives of (its) choice" has been impaired and claims that "its ability *to influence* elections" has been impaired.[247]

The obvious problem with the concept of "minority influenced" districts, however, was that it quickly devolved into a slippery slope. Was a 50% minority district sufficient to influence an election? 30%? 10%? 1%? The concept, dangled in a theoretical vacuum, provided no benchmark for the Commission in a sea of arguable "minority influenced" districts. In Allegheny, Philadelphia, Lancaster, and Dauphin Counties, a host of putative "influence" districts could be twisted, stretched, and punched out of the map, while destroying communities of interest and political boundaries along the way. The Commission approached this issue gingerly, recognizing that the law was undeveloped and unsettled.

A number of lower court decisions had rejected the notion of "minority influenced" districts as an unworkable nightmare never envisioned by the Voting

---

[245] *See* REAPPORTIONMENT LAW: THE 1990's, *supra* note 224, at 60-61.

[246] *See* NAACP REDISTRICTING PROJECT HANDBOOK 13-14 (1991) (State Archives).

[247] *Gingles*, 478 U.S. at 89-90 n.1 (O'Connor, J., concurring) (citations omitted). Indeed, the majority in *Gingles* also raised, and left open, the question. *See id.* at 46 n.12.

Rights Act.[248] At the same time, some commentators predicted that the Supreme Court would embrace the requirement of "influence" districts under Section 2 when the time came.[249] A "middle-ground" was also developing. A three-judge panel in the federal district court of Ohio had just held that minority plaintiffs did not have to comprise a majority in a reconfigured district in order to establish a Section 2 violation.[250] Rather, in a 2-to-1 opinion, the panel held that plaintiffs had met their burden of demonstrating an ability to elect a candidate of their choice, albeit with fewer than 50% of the population. Here, in the court's view, the minority proportion could do more than influence, it could elect:

> In a reconfigured district, plaintiffs will constitute nearly one-third of the voting age population and about half of the usual Democratic vote. Therefore, the Democratic Party and its candidates will be forced to be sensitive to the minority population by virtue of that population's size. … Since black voters consistently vote eighty to ninety percent Democratic and white voters vote consistently almost fifty percent Democratic, we find that plaintiffs could elect a candidate of their choice, although not necessarily of their race, in a reconfigured district.[251]

Thus, the court reasoned, it was unnecessary to determine whether a pure "minority influenced" district would be mandated under the Act.

Through this somewhat curious reasoning, the *Armour* panel had created a theory midway between endorsing and rejecting a pure "minority-influenced" rationale. Even if the minority group was far below a 65% threshold (or indeed a 50% numerical majority), one might argue that Section 2 required the creation of such a new district if one could demonstrate that the minority group constituted a "swing vote" and might dictate the outcome of an election. As to the obvious problem that *Gingles* had required minority plaintiffs to demonstrate that they constituted a *majority* in the proposed district, the *Armour* panel simply suggested that this aspect of *Gingles* related only to multimember districts, not to single-member district elections.[252]

The net effect of the decisions and commentary regarding "minority influenced" districts was that the Pennsylvania Commission was left to guesswork and conjecture, as was the rest of the country. The Commission remained sensitive to the creation of such districts, whether mandated by federal law or not. The Chairman generally followed a path of logic that he should entertain the notion of creating "influence districts" on a sliding scale, giving increased weight to this notion as the minority percentages grew higher in a particular district.

D. Can Minorities Be Aggregated?

The final unresolved twist on the Voting Rights Act which presented itself vividly in Pennsylvania, particularly in Philadelphia, was whether different minority groups could be combined or "aggregated" in order to reach the magic number

---

[248] *See, e.g.*, McNeil v. Springfield Park Dist., 851 F.2d 937, 947 (7th Cir. 1988), *cert. denied*, 490 U.S. 1031 (1989); Hastert v. State Bd. of Elections, 777 F. Supp. 634, 655 (N.D. Ill. 1991); Skorepa v. City of Chula Vista, 723 F. Supp. 1384, 1391-92 (S.D. Cal. 1989).

[249] *See, e.g.*, Pamela S. Karlan, *Maps and Misreadings: The Role of Geographic Compactness in Racial Vote Dilution Litigation*, 24 HARV. C.R.-C.L. L. REV. 173, 206 & n.129 (1989).

[250] Armour v. Ohio, 775 F. Supp. 1044 (N.D. Ohio 1991).

[251] *Id.* at 1059-60.

[252] *Id.* at 1051-52.

required for a majority-minority district (i.e. something close to 65%). This question became relevant because African-American and Latino voters existed side-by-side in a number of communities, most notably in the center of Philadelphia. Thus, the issue presented itself whether these two distinct minority groups could (or should) be lumped together to create a single, larger minority seat.

The case law on aggregation was murky at best. A number of courts had held that where the *Gingles* criteria were otherwise met, different minority groups could be aggregated in order to constitute a single "minority" under Section 2 of the Act. For instance, in *Concerned Citizens of Hardee County v. Hardee County Board of Commissioners*,[253] the Eleventh Circuit Court of Appeals had held that African-Americans and Latinos could be combined to constitute a single minority for purposes of asserting a violation of the Voting Rights Act, if they could establish that they behaved in a politically cohesive manner.[254] On the flip side, a number of courts had held that distinct minority groups could *not be* aggregated, where the minority groups failed to demonstrate the political cohesiveness required by *Gingles*.[255]

In sum, there existed a powder keg full of Voting Rights Act issues for the Commission to consider in 1991. The Commission had to face all of these issues before placing its imprimatur on a Final Plan.

---

[253] 906 F.2d 524 (11th Cir. 1990).

[254] *Id.* at 526; *see also* Campos v. City of Baytown, 840 F.2d 1240, 1245 (5th Cir. 1988), *cert. denied*, 109 S. Ct. 3213 (1989); League of United Latin Am. Citizens v. Midland Indep. Sch. Dist., 812 F.2d 1494 (5th Cir. 1987), *vacated*, 829 F.2d 546 (5th Cir. 1987).

[255] *See* Brewer v. Ham, 876 F.2d 448 (5th Cir. 1989) (African-American, Asian, and Latino voters); Overton v. City of Austin, 871 F.2d 529 (5th Cir. 1989) (African-American and Hispanic voters).

VIII.
A STORM OF OTHER LEGAL ISSUES

The Federal Voting Rights Act concerns, although quickly predominating in the Pennsylvania Reapportionment of 1991, were not the only legal issues confronting the Commission as it moved into the final stages of its work. As already mentioned, the difficulties of achieving one-person-one-vote, although greatly reduced with the advent of computer programs, nonetheless mandated constant attention as the Commission considered proposals for a Final Plan. Likewise, the requirements of Article II, Section 16 of the Pennsylvania Constitution — compactness, contiguity, and maintenance of political boundaries — remained an ever-present concern for the Commission members and their staffs. Finally, the question of merging two senate seats, and the Chairman's concern for maintaining "political fairness" in the process, presented additional puzzles never before tackled in one lump by a Commission.

A. Merging "Odd" and "Even" Numbered Senate Seats

Chairman Cindrich's decision to merge one odd and one even numbered senate seat (the 43rd and the 44th) in western Pennsylvania to deal with population losses produced dramatic political, as well as legal, consequences.[256] The decision yielded political consequences because it would result in one incumbent senator, Senator Frank Pecora, a Republican, living outside his old district and the newly reconstituted 43rd District being represented by Senator Michael Dawida, a Democrat. Likewise, the decision produced legal consequences because no precise precedent existed to determine what should happen to the even-numbered district — and its incumbent senator — once collapsed and moved across the state in midterm.

Pennsylvania statutory law provides for staggered four-year state senatorial terms.[257] All odd-numbered districts hold elections in the same year (1988, 1992, etc.), while the even-numbered districts hold elections at staggered two-year intervals (1990, 1994, etc.). Thus, the merger of the 43rd Senatorial District, which was scheduled for an election in 1992, and the 44th Senatorial District, which was not scheduled for an election until 1994, raised a novel legal problem: What happened to Senator Pecora once the 44th District moved east?

These were perplexing questions. The Pennsylvania Supreme Court in *Butcher v. Bloom* had held that an elected officeholder had no vested tenure in that position.[258] At the same time, the *Butcher* Court, in adopting its own reapportionment plan, had required that elections take place in all fifty districts. Was it permissible for the Commission to cut short one senator's term without triggering the cost and labor of an election in all fifty districts? A smattering of cases throughout the United States suggested that a reapportionment body might possess the authority

---

[256] As discussed previously, Chairman Cindrich's directive was actually that one Democratic and one Republican senatorial district in western Pennsylvania should be merged. *See* Transcript of Legislative Reapportionment Commission Public Hearing 20-28 (Sept. 25, 1991) (State Archives). The Democrats proposed merging the seats of Senator Pecora and Senator Dawida; the Republicans did not offer a counter-proposal and instead maintained that two Democratic seats representing the greatest population losses should be merged.

[257] *See* 22 PA. CONS. STAT. ANN. §2209. *See also* PA. CONST. art. 2, §3; PA. CONST. sched. 1, §4.

[258] 420 Pa. 305, 310 n.10, 216 A.2d 457, 459 n.10 (1966).

to cut short a legislator's term as part of the necessary reshuffling of districts.[259] Chief Counsel Harmelin advised the Commission that it was most likely within the inherent powers of the Commission under Article II, Section 17 of the Pennsylvania Constitution to renumber seats as part of its reapportionment duties; thus the move of the 44th seat across the state would most likely be defensible in court. However, these issues were far from clear-cut.

Finally, the Commission knew that the Lieutenant Governor possessed statutory power to call a special election to fill vacant senatorial seats.[260] This provided solace in the sense that a mechanism existed to fill the 44th senatorial seat if the seat were moved and declared vacant (assuming the Senate refused to seat Senator Pecora). Thus, the odd-even cycle would remain undisturbed. All of these factors satisfied the Chairman (over objection by the Senate Republicans) that it was responsible to allow the merger of the 43rd and the 44th Districts. However, the decision remained a thorny one.

B. Considerations of "Political Fairness"

Chairman Cindrich placed significant emphasis, both in public debate and in private meetings with reapportionment staff, on the need to maintain a modicum of political fairness in allowing the redistricting map to take shape. Much of this concern was framed by a 1991 Report prepared by Dr. Donald E. Stokes, Dean of the Princeton University Woodrow Wilson School of Public International Affairs. Dean Stokes had been appointed by the New Jersey Supreme Court to serve as the "neutral" member of an otherwise political New Jersey Apportionment Commission in 1981 and had recorded his observations and findings in a monograph entitled *Legislative Reapportionment in New Jersey.*[261] Dean Stokes, the *de facto* chairman of the New Jersey Board, had placed great emphasis upon maintaining fairness between the political parties. To aid in this goal, Dean Stokes had developed simple graphing techniques to determine whether a reapportionment plan maintained the parties' expected balance of power given voter registration, past voting patterns, and other basic factors.[262]

Early in the Pennsylvania process, Chairman Cindrich requested that LDPC tabulate data regarding past legislative elections, as well as voter registration data. This information would allow a simulation of mock elections in the proposed legislative districts for purposes of determining if the Commission had maintained relative fairness between the political parties. This simple check allowed the Chairman to satisfy himself, at least with respect to major decisions, that the ultimate reapportionment plan would not represent a dramatic shift in the existing balance of power for either political party.

The merger of one Democratic and one Republican Senate seat in Allegheny County provides the most dramatic example of the Chairman's cognizance of "political fairness." As Chairman Cindrich stated in public hearings on this matter, it did not seem to achieve political fairness if an area comprised of approxi-

---

[259] *See, e.g.,* Ferrell v. Oklahoma, 339 F. Supp. 73 (W.D. Okla.), *aff'd,* 406 U.S. 939 (1972); *In re* Apportionment Law, 414 So. 2d 1040 (Fla. 1982); Legislature of Cal. v. Reinecke, 516 P.2d 6 (Cal. 1973).

[260] *See* 25 PA. CONS. STAT. ANN. §2278; *see also* PA. CONST. art. II, §2. The presiding officer of the Senate is the Lieutenant Governor, *see* Marston v. Kline, 8 Pa. Cmwlth. 143, 145, 301 A.2d 393, 394 (1973), and thus is vested with this power.

[261] DONALD E. STOKES, LEGISLATIVE REAPPORTIONMENT IN NEW JERSEY (1991).

[262] *Id.* at 10-18.

mately 70% Democratic voters were re-configured to create three "safe" Senate seats for the Republicans and three "safe" seats for the Democrats.[263] Rather, political fairness seemed to dictate that if the 44th Senatorial Seat were moved east into a predominantly Republican area, creating a "new" Republican seat in that area of population growth, the merger in the west should reflect the heavily Democratic composition in that area. The merger of one Democratic and one Republican seat in Allegheny County would result in four predominantly Democratic seats and two predominantly Republican seats, a result which more fairly reflected the existing balance of power in that part of the map. Graphs produced by LDPC using the Stokes' model confirmed the relative fairness of the preliminary plan statewide, at least in the Chairman's mind.

Senator Loeper, the Senate Republican Commission member, registered his vigorous dissent to this approach. In Senator Loeper's opinion, population shifts since the last reapportionment warranted that *two* Democrats should be merged in Allegheny County. Senator Loeper argued that the districts which had lost the greatest amount of population should be the first districts to be collapsed. This proposal would have resulted in three incumbent Democrats and three incumbent Republicans retaining their seats in Allegheny County.[264] In the end, however, the Chairman rejected this logic. He believed that it would result in a skewed balance of power in a region with 70% democratic voters. Although the issue of whether it was legitimate for the Chairman to consider "political fairness" was hotly debated, with the Senate Republicans charging that this constituted "political gerrymandering" in violation of the United States Supreme Court's decision in *Davis v. Bandemer*,[265] the Chairman remained insistent and the *Stokes Report* left its imprimatur on the Final Plan.

---

[263] *See* Transcript of Legislative Reapportionment Commission Public Hearing 25-27 (Sept. 25, 1991) (State Archives).

[264] *Id.* at 8-12. Senator Loeper noted that all three districts in Allegheny County which were then represented by Republicans enjoyed significant Democratic registration margins, making none of those three seats "safe" Republican seats. In fact, the predecessor of each of the three Republican incumbents had been Democrats.

[265] 478 U.S. 109 (1986). This issue was raised by the Senate Republicans both in public hearings, *see* Transcript of Legislative Reapportionment Commission Public Hearing 8-12 (Sept. 25, 1991) (State Archives), as well as in subsequent legal challenges to the Final Plan. *See, e.g.*, Petition for Review, F. Joseph Loeper, No. 201 E.D. Misc. Dkt. 1991, 7 (Dec. 16, 1991) (State Archives).

IX.
A FINAL PLAN IS FORGED

A. Groundwork for a Final Plan (Long Nights)

In the swirl of discussion over these dramatic legal issues, including the Voting Rights Act and other novel problems, the Commission moved forward to forge a Final Plan. Not only did the public hearings and written public comments influence the Commission, but the Commission for the first time in history retained an expert to advise it in molding a plan that would comply with the Federal Voting Rights Act.

The Commission decided, via its Counsel, to hire Dr. Richard L. Engstrom of the University of New Orleans, a nationally-recognized expert in Voting Rights Act analysis. This decision was significant for several reasons. First, Dr. Engstrom was well qualified as a neutral scholar, having represented minority groups, the U.S. Department of Justice, state and local governments, and reapportionment bodies — virtually every side of the equation in voting rights suits throughout the United States.[266] Rather than looking for a "hired gun," the Commission intentionally sought out Dr. Engstrom because of his independent track record. If anything, his principal emphasis had been on representing African-Americans, Latinos, and other minority groups who had challenged reapportionment plans as violative of their statutory and constitutional rights. Most important, the Pennsylvania Commission decided to retain Dr. Engstrom *prior* to adoption of the Final Plan to aid in *formulating* that plan. This approach stood in marked contrast to the approach of those states that had adopted reapportionment plans first and sought experts to defend those plans only after the redistricting plan was *fait accompli* and facing challenges in court.

At the request of the Chairman and Chief Counsel Harmelin, Dr. Engstrom gathered data relating to a host of statewide and local elections in Pennsylvania over the past decade and tabulated that data to determine whether the *Gingles* criteria were at least arguably satisfied in areas of the highest minority concentrations — Philadelphia, Pittsburgh, Harrisburg, and Lancaster County. By conducting "ecological regression analysis," the methodology commonly accepted in the field and utilized in *Gingles* itself, Dr. Engstrom provided insight as to (1) whether geographically compact majority African-American or Latino districts could be created in these key areas; (2) whether minority voters were politically cohesive in the sense that they generally voted for the same candidates; and (3) whether the minorities' candidates of choice had been routinely defeated by racially polarized bloc voting. In other words, Dr. Engstrom provided an early snapshot of the three principal *Gingles* criteria.

Of equal importance, Dr. Engstrom provided guidance as to the approximate percentage of African-American or Latino voters in particular districts that were likely to elect "candidates of choice," given the minority groups' voting age population, voter registration, and past performance in elections.[267] Dr. Engstrom's

---

[266] *See* Vita, Richard L. Engstrom (June, 1991) (State Archives). Dr. Engstrom's work was cited by the U.S. Supreme Court in *Gingles. See* 478 U.S. at 46 n.11.

[267] Dr. Engstrom's analysis, although considered confidential attorney-client work product in these early stages, was later explained and documented at great length during his testimony in the subsequent Philadelphia voting rights suit entitled *Harrison v. Pennsylvania Reapportionment Commission. See infra* part XI. *See also* The Pennsylvania Legislative Reapportionment Commission's Post-Hearing Brief (Apr. 13, 1992) (summarizing Engstrom testimony) (State Archives).

data was critical, particularly in Philadelphia, in deciding whether districts slightly under the 65% "rule of thumb" would be viable and thus allow the Commission to create more minority districts than those carved out in the preliminary plan.

Although Dr. Engstrom did not seek to provide definitive answers to the Commission at this early stage — the data at this juncture was incomplete at best[268] — Dr. Engstrom did supply the Chairman and Chief Counsel with invaluable pictures of the legal terrain that would evolve if a voting rights suit were brought. First, Dr. Engstrom concluded that a voting rights plaintiff would probably not face great difficulty in establishing the three basic *Gingles* criteria in Philadelphia, Pittsburgh, or Harrisburg; indeed, Engstrom concluded that this hurdle would be an easy one in most urban centers throughout the United States, even without performing a detailed analysis of the data. Second, and perhaps more important in influencing the work of the Commission, Dr. Engstrom found a surprisingly high cohesiveness and voter turnout among African-American voters in Philadelphia. Indeed, the voter turnout among African-Americans in many cases was *higher* than the voter turnout among whites, particularly when African-American candidates were running for office. This meant, in Engstrom's opinion, that a percentage significantly lower than the 65% "rule of thumb" would allow African-Americans to elect candidates of choice. Therefore, in Engstrom's view, the Voting Rights Act supported, if not mandated, dropping the "rule of thumb" proportion to approximately 60% and creating additional minority House and Senate seats in Philadelphia within that range.

Finally, Dr. Engstrom expressed serious reservations about "aggregating" African-American and Latino voters in Philadelphia. It was unclear to him that these two minority groups voted cohesively at all. All of this advice, communicated initially to the Chairman and Chief Counsel, was passed along to the other Commission members, sparking the greatest internal debate among staff and rival political parties since the 1991 Commission had been constituted.

The Executive Director of the Commission maintained direct contact with the national office of the NAACP in Baltimore, the Philadelphia Latino Voting Rights Committee, the Puerto Rican Legal Defense and Education Fund in New York, and other minority groups who had supplied written comments to the Preliminary Plan or offered alternative maps to better ensure minority representation. The Executive Director also recorded and tabulated thousands of letters, faxes, phone calls, signatures on petitions, and other input from citizens and organizations throughout Pennsylvania. The Commission organized this input by county and region, as well as by topic. The original comments were circulated to each Commission member and staff, along with a summary prepared by the Executive Director. The Chairman and the Executive Director then met for two days in Harrisburg with staff members to consider which comments were meritorious and feasible, and which might warrant incorporation into the Final Plan.[269]

On November 11, 1991, the Commission met with the intention of voting on a Final Plan of reapportionment. The Chairman announced, however, that "there were substantial disagreements about what changes, if any, should be made and where."[270] The Chairman also made public that he had directed each caucus to present a plan containing *four* majority-minority Senate seats in the city of Phila-

---

[268] *Id.*

[269] *See* Transcript of Legislative Reapportionment Commission Public Meeting 14-16 (Nov. 15, 1991) (State Archives).

[270] *See* Transcript of Legislative Reapportionment Commission Public Meeting 3 (Nov. 11, 1991) (State Archives).

delphia (rather than the three minority seats reflected in the Preliminary Plan), which the Senate Democrats had failed to carry out.[271] The meeting was therefore recessed for four days.

On Friday, November 15, 1991, again after staying up most of the night in an effort to hammer out last-minute changes with staffs, the Chairman convened a historic meeting at which a Final Plan of reapportionment was adopted with bipartisan support from the Democratic and Republican House members. Both members from the Senate would vote against the Plan, in an interesting twist of politics and fate.

B. A Vote is Reached

When the meeting of November 15th was convened, the House staffs and the Chairman had reached a tentative agreement regarding an acceptable Final House Plan.[272] Significantly, at the direction of Chairman Cindrich, the new plan included an increase in majority-minority districts in Philadelphia. The revised plan encompassed twelve minority House districts in Philadelphia, including one majority Hispanic seat (62.3% — the 180th), and an additional seat with a strong Latino influence (30.6% — the 179th) in the region that the Latino community had indicated was its principal area of growth.[273] Following these and other changes, the Chairman and House commission members were generally satisfied with the proposed Final Plan for the House.

In the Senate, however, a wide and seemingly unbridgeable schism had developed. Senator Mellow, representing the Democratic caucus, expressed concern that increasing the number of minority seats in Philadelphia, as the Chairman had directed, would in reality diminish the influence of black leaders in the Senate. Reading from a letter submitted by Senator Roxanne Jones, the incumbent African-American senator representing the 3rd District, Mellow concluded that "[t]hese plans would further segregate the African-American community from the body politic of Philadelphia."[274] In Senator Mellow's view, it was preferable to maintain the existing configuration of three minority seats. The 4th District, represented by Senator Allyson Schwartz, would continue to include a heavy minority influence.[275] Senator Mellow therefore proposed a map maintaining three minority senate seats in Philadelphia; this proposal, however, was defeated.[276]

Senator Loeper, on behalf of the Senate Republicans, then introduced seven different plans in an effort to convince the Chairman that he should abandon his proposed Final Plan. Most of the plans introduced by Senator Loeper would have created four majority-minority seats in Philadelphia by aggregating, or combining, African-American citizens (54.9%) and Latino citizens (25.6%) in the 3rd District, while creating a 2nd District which was much more favorable to Republican

---

[271] *Id.* at 3-4.

[272] *See* Transcript of Legislative Reapportionment Commission Public Meetings 20 (Nov. 15, 1991) (State Archives).

[273] *Id.* at 106-09.

[274] *Id.* at 35-37.

[275] In this regard, the Chairman indicated that the Commission had received letters from the Legislative Black Caucus and certain black clergy of Philadelphia, opposing increased minority seats in the House and Senate in Philadelphia. *Id.* at 48-50. However, it should be noted that the Legislative Black Caucus had informally withdrawn its objection to creating a fourth minority seat in Philadelphia, and had worked with the NAACP, the Chairman, and the Executive Director in formulating a plan which would be acceptable to the Chairman and the black community.

[276] *Id.* at 57-68.

The Chairman presides over executive session of the full Commission, prior to a public hearing on the Preliminary Plan.

Representative Allen G. Kukovich (D., Westmoreland County) consults with staff.

Representative John M. Perzel (R., Philadelphia) consults with House Republican staff member Stephen Dull.

Senate Democratic Floor Leader Robert J. Mellow (D., Lackawanna County) and his staff.

The Chairman consults with Chief Counsel.

Senate Republicans ponder a thorny legal issue.

The Chairman and Executive Director caucus informally with House staff members — Stephen Dull and Scott Casper — to hash over preliminary maps.

Senator Loeper with outside legal counsel David Norcross, who would later argue Republican challenges in the Pennsylvania Supreme Court.

The full Commission convenes for a public hearing.

Senate Majority Leader F. Joseph Loeper (R., Delaware County) with key advisors (left to right) David Norcross, Stephen MacNett and David Woods.

Chairman Robert J. Cindrich and Executive Director Ken Gormley absorb testimony at public hearing.

Chief Counsel Stephen J. Harmelin drafts a proposed Resolution, as Chairman Cindrich watches on.

A tense moment during debate.

Senator Mellow and his key advisors: Mark McKillop (left) and legal counsel C. J. Hafner (right).

House Democratic staff member Scott Casper displays a proposed majority African-American district in Philadelphia, as the Chairman and Executive Director watch boundaries take shape on the computer terminal.

Chairman Robert J. Cindrich shares a laugh with Senate Democratic staffer Mark McKillop.

Senator Mellow unveils a proposed Democratic map for Philadelphia.

Representative Kukovich and his principal advisor, Scott Casper.

Senators Mellow and Loeper make a final effort to forge a deal, but fail to reach common ground. Both Senators ultimately voted against the Final Plan, for distinct reasons.

House Republican staff member Stephen Dull makes a point while House Democratic staffer, Scott Casper, listens carefully.

Senate Democratic Floor Leader Robert J. Mellow (D., Lackawanna County) is interviewed by the Capitol press corps after voting against the Final Plan.

Representative Thomas P. Gannon (R., Delaware County), sitting in for Representative John M. Perzel (R., Philadelphia) to cast a critical vote on the Final Plan. With him is Republican staffer Stephen Dull.

Chief Counsel Stephen J. Harmelin (center) reviews trial strategy with co-counsel Laurence Shtasel and Barbara Brown Krancer. Shtasel and Krancer handled the Federal Voting Rights Act litigation in Philadelphia, and also presented arguments in the Pennsylvania Supreme Court.

The Chairman and Executive Director pose in front of the State Capitol, after nearly a year's worth of reapportionment work.

Commission Counsel Barbara Brown Krancer and Laurence Shtasel meet in front of federal court in Philadelphia prior to Voting Rights Act trial.

Executive Director of the Legislative Data Processing Center, Al Stockslager, consults with the Reapportionment Commission's Executive Secretary, Barbara Butterfield Janecko.

Photographs by Jim Haberski and Will Ketner

candidates. The Chairman, who constituted the swing vote, rejected all of these proposals out of concern that (1) Dr. Engstrom was uncertain that African-Americans and Latinos could be aggregated because they did not vote cohesively and (2) the Republican plans would split the Latino community between two districts, with one of those districts dominated by African-Americans, rather than moving most Latino voters into a single district, the 2nd, which represented their area of growth.[277]

Senator Loeper also introduced plans which would change the configuration of, or flip the numbers of, the 43rd and 44th Districts. The net result of these proposals would be to preserve Senator Pecora's seat in Allegheny County.[278] The Chairman also rejected these proposals out of concern that political fairness dictated the merging of a Democrat and Republican in Allegheny County, moving the even-numbered seat east, and conducting an election in 1992, rather than 1994, so that voters of the merged 43rd District could select the candidate whom they considered most qualified.[279] Moreover, the mechanism of a special election would be available in the new 44th District.[280]

Senator Loeper next proposed a map which would keep the city of Philadelphia whole, eliminating the disgruntlement of the citizens of Lower Moreland and Cheltenham Townships, but driving up the percentage population deviation to approximately 7% and aggregating African-Americans and Latinos into a single district.[281] The Chairman acknowledged that there was some appeal to the approach of keeping Philadelphia whole in order to avoid breaking into suburbs outside the city. However, the Chairman was skeptical whether the one-person-one-vote principle would (or should) tolerate deviations as high as 7% to 10% when the Senate deviations could otherwise be kept to a tiny fraction.[282] On that basis, the Chairman also rejected this proposal.

Finally, Senator Loeper proposed a plan for Philadelphia which would incorporate the Democrats' *own plan* for that city and result in only three minority seats.[283] Much to the surprise of the Chairman and many other observers, Senator Mellow now joined the Chairman in voting against his own "Democratic plan," noting that it would vary the ultimate scheme outside of Philadelphia.[284]

After these alternatives were rejected, the Chairman called for a vote on the plan originally on the table, which represented the House plan (acceptable to both caucuses in the House) and a Senate plan created at the direction of the Chairman. This plan created four minority senate seats in Philadelphia, in percentages consistent with the advice of the Commission's voting rights expert, as follows: 3rd District (60.63%); 4th District (61.52%); 7th District (61.81%); and 8th District (60.14%). The Chairman's plan put the bulk of the Latino population (23%) in a single district, the 2nd District, which corresponded to that community's area of growth. The plan sought to accomplish these goals, according to Chairman Cindrich, without dramatically disturbing the dominant Democratic configuration of

---

[277] *Id.* at 23-27, 74-80.

[278] *Id.* at 20-30, 89-90, 94-95.

[279] *Id.* at 29.

[280] *Id.* at 113-14.

[281] *Id.* at 81-88; *see also* Transcript of Legislative Reapportionment Commission Meeting 3-6 (Nov. 11, 1991) (regarding the proposal to keep Philadelphia whole) (State Archives).

[282] Transcript of Legislative Reapportionment Commission Hearing 84-87 (Nov. 15, 1991) (State Archives).

[283] *Id.* at 95-100.

[284] *Id.* at 97-98.

Philadelphia as it existed.[285] Finally, the Chairman's proposal created two minority House districts in Pittsburgh, as well as one senate seat in Pittsburgh that contained approximately 35% black population while preserving the boundaries of a host of municipalities.[286]

In a final volley of debate, Senator Loeper charged that the Chairman's plan amounted to a "world class gerrymander," asserting that it created "not a single classic majority-minority district in the city of Philadelphia."[287] Senator Loeper also challenged the merging and moving of the 44th District, stating that it was a "flip-flop [that] only serves to impose political disadvantage on a district that's held by a Republican, and such late-breaking political mischief serves no political purpose and discredits the work of this entire Commission."[288]

Chairman Cindrich defended the plan based upon its consistency with the advice of Dr. Engstrom, the Commission's voting rights expert, as well as his own sense of "conscience." The Chairman stated:

> I have done what I perceived to be my job, and I think it is my job to
> be the person who looks out for interests that would not otherwise be
> protected. It is the legitimate function of the political parties, both Re-
> publican and Democrat, to press their interests and to press them hard,
> to gain political advantage where they can, and it's my job to see that
> the voter is protected. It's my job to see that the minorities are pro-
> tected and that the Constitution is adhered to. And in doing so, that
> sometimes doesn't make the parties happy at all.[289]

The Chairman also declared that the test of political fairness would be met by the plan. As to a potential lawsuit by Senator Pecora, the Chairman stated: "I'm sure that he and his lawyer know where the courthouse is located."[290]

With that, more than 150 days after the Commission had begun its work, Chairman Cindrich called for a vote on the Final Plan of reapportionment. Senators Loeper and Mellow voted against the Plan, for the reasons advanced above. Representatives Kukovich, a Democrat, and Thomas P. Gannon, a Republican from Delaware County serving as proxy for Representative Perzel, who was out of town, voted in favor of the Plan.[291]

Chairman Cindrich then cast his vote in favor of the Plan, solidifying an unusual majority. After announcing that any aggrieved citizen could file an appeal directly with the Pennsylvania Supreme Court within thirty days of that date, the Chairman adjourned the meeting. The 1991 Pennsylvania Legislative Reapportionment Commission had adopted a Final Plan through a bipartisan, split vote consisting of two House members and the Chairman.

Just as the Chairman returned to his office in the Capitol, after filing the Final Plan of reapportionment, he was besieged by newspaper reporters who wanted to know why one prominent candidate for the state Senate, former Republican State Chairman Clifford L. Jones of Cumberland County, had been "drawn out" of his home district in the late-night revisions to the Plan, making him incapable of run-

---

[285] *Id.* at 102-09. The Senate Republicans asserted the Plan did not disturb the dominant Democratic configuration in Philadelphia but instead enhanced it.

[286] *Id.* at 108.

[287] *Id.* at 110.

[288] *Id.* at 111.

[289] *Id.* at 103-04.

[290] *Id.* at 112-13.

[291] *Id.* at 115.

ning for office in 1992.[292] Thus began the onslaught of challenges and complaints — some of them surprises, others not — which would culminate in a long string of hearings before the Pennsylvania Supreme Court on January 25, 1992. In the meantime, the Final Plan was duly published throughout the Commonwealth, making its way onto thousands of maps distributed across Pennsylvania.

---

[292] Jones had announced his candidacy on the local courthouse steps just three hours earlier. *See* Clifford L. Jones v. Pennsylvania Legislative Reapportionment Comm'n, No. 4:CV-92-0729, Complaint at Para. 1-4 (M.D. Pa., Mar. 5, 1992) (State Archives).

X.
PROCEEDINGS BEFORE THE
PENNSYLVANIA SUPREME COURT

A. The Challenges are Filed

Twenty-five challenges were filed against the Final Plan within the thirty-day period prescribed by the Constitution. These included suits by disgruntled legislators, suits by disgruntled would-be candidates such as Clifford Jones, suits under the Voting Rights Act (including one by Senator F. Joseph Loeper), suits by Senator Frank Pecora and other legislators who had lost their seats, suits by individual citizens and civic associations, and suits by voters from Cheltenham and Lower Moreland Townships who had been mingled with the city of Philadelphia in proposed new Senate seats. Not a single minority organization that had vigorously participated in the public comment period during the reapportionment process filed a lawsuit. Informally, representatives of these groups informed the Executive Director that they were satisfied with the Plan. Yet even without complaints by participating minority organizations, the challenges mounted.

The pre-hearing procedures within the Pennsylvania Supreme Court were murky at best. The Pennsylvania Constitution provides only that any aggrieved party "may file an appeal from the final plan directly to the Supreme Court within thirty days after the filing thereof."[293] If the Final Plan is found to be contrary to law, "the Supreme Court shall issue an order remanding the plan to the Commission and directing the Commission to reapportion the Commonwealth in a manner not inconsistent with such order."[294]

Other than this broad directive, the Constitution is silent as to the procedures to be followed in the state's highest court. This posed certain logistical problems, since the Supreme Court is geared almost exclusively to hearing *appellate* cases in which a factual record, depositions, discovery, and a trial transcript have been developed in the lower courts. In the case of the myriad reapportionment appeals, however, it was not clear what data, if any, the parties could rely upon in challenging the Plan, other than the naked reapportionment plan itself and transcripts of public hearings. No real procedure existed for developing facts, reducing them to the form of testimony or exhibits, or presenting them to the Pennsylvania Supreme Court. Nor would time allow the sort of wide-ranging discovery that typically marks modern litigation. This was particularly true given the need for the Court to accept or reject a reapportionment plan in time for Commonwealth elections to move forward without delay.

Consequently, the pre-hearing skirmishing that occurred before the Supreme Court considered the Final Plan was sporadic and ill-defined. Petitions for review were filed according to the generic rules of the Pennsylvania Supreme Court.[295] Some petitions were prepared by attorneys; others were handwritten or typed as letters or crude pleadings prepared by the petitioners themselves. The Commission's counsel filed preliminary objections to a handful of petitions, particularly where the petitions were unintelligible or raised facially improper claims. Otherwise, the Commission sought to err on the side of allowing the Court to hear all

---

[293] PA. CONST. art. II, §17(d).
[294] *Id.*
[295] *See* Pa. R. App. P. §§1501 *et seq. See also* Pa. R. App. P. §3321.

challenges and filed a lengthy consolidated answer responding to all twenty-five petitions, paragraph by paragraph.[296] A sprinkling of petitions sought to take depositions or otherwise engage in pre-hearing discovery; these ultimately languished and became moot as a result of the Court's failure to acknowledge or address them.

B. A Marathon Hearing is Scheduled

On January 21, 1992, as petitions, replies, and extraneous motions before the Supreme Court continued to mount, the Commission received a telephone call from the Prothonotary of the Pennsylvania Supreme Court advising that oral argument would be held on all twenty-five Petitions that Saturday morning, January 25, 1992, in Philadelphia. The Court had divided the petitions into three broad clusters, based upon the nature of the challenges. It had assigned a one-hour time slot to each cluster. This gave the Commission's Chief Counsel, Stephen J. Harmelin, and his two associate counsel, Laurence S. Shtasel and Barbara Brown Krancer, exactly four days to complete a comprehensive brief that covered all twenty-five lawsuits and prepare for oral argument.

In addressing the mountain of petitions and hastily-drafted briefs, the Commission's counsel adopted the approach of seeking to assist the Court in a somewhat detached and neutral fashion, just as the Solicitor General of the United States is often called upon to wear a dual hat as litigant and advisor to the U.S. Supreme Court. Rather than embrace an aggressive, bent-on-prevailing-on-every-issue approach which would have been the norm for modern litigation, the Chairman and Chief Counsel chose to provide the Court with as much information as possible so that the Court could make rational decisions. Transcripts of the public reapportionment hearings and meetings were quickly provided to the Court for background. Where Counsel and the Chairman lacked sufficient information to admit or deny allegations raised in the pleadings of petitioners, the Commission attempted to acknowledge this fact openly and to address the petitions based upon whatever legitimate legal grounds existed. Not only was this approach meant to foster the trust of the Court, but it also reflected the belief of the Chairman himself that the Commission was acting not as a litigant in the typical sense, but as a representative of all citizens of the Commonwealth. Thus, if the Reapportionment Plan was legally defective in any way, the Chairman believed, the Court should have a chance to determine this for itself so that any defect could be corrected.

On paper, Counsel for the Commission broke down the challenges into seven major categories.[297] First, a number of petitioners alleged that the Final Plan failed to create districts "as nearly equal in population as possible," in violation of the one-person-one-vote standard. Typical of such complaints was the petition of Spring Hill Civic League in Allegheny County. This petition alleged that the population deviation between the 19th and 20th House Districts in Pittsburgh was unconstitutionally large and that the Spring Hill neighborhood should be consolidated into a single legislative district to make these two abutting districts more compact and closer to the ideal population norm.[298]

---

[296] *See* Consolidated Answer of Respondent Pennsylvania Legislative Reapportionment Commission to Petitions (Jan. 13, 1991) (State Archives).

[297] *See* Brief of Respondent Pennsylvania Legislative Reapportionment Commission, No. 190 E.D. Misc. Dkt. 1991 Consolidated (Jan. 25, 1992) (State Archives).

[298] *Id.* at 9; *see also* Petition for Review of Spring Hill Civic League and Darlene Harris, No. 133 W.D. Misc. Dkt. (Dec. 12, 1991) (State Archives).

In a related vein, a number of petitioners alleged that the Final Plan created districts which were not "compact and contiguous" as required by Article II, Section 16 of the Pennsylvania Constitution. Typical of these claims were the petitions of Lawrence Roberts, Thomas Rabbitt Zajac, and South Union Township, all of whom contended that the 49th House District in Fayette County resembled a "monster" or an "hour glass" shape. The petitions alleged that these strained configurations were designed to achieve political expediencies and were thus rendered unconstitutional.[299]

Third, numerous petitioners alleged that the Final Plan had improperly split political subdivisions, including cities, counties, wards, and townships, in violation of Article II, Section 16 of the Pennsylvania Constitution. Typical of this group was the petition of Westmoreland County Democratic Committee Chairman Dante G. Bertani, who alleged in his pleadings that the Final Plan unnecessarily split Westmoreland County into seven senatorial districts.[300]

Fourth, several notable petitioners raised "political gerrymandering" claims, challenging the Commission's motives in drawing certain districts and claiming that lines were intentionally skewed to protect incumbents. Clifford Jones, the high-profile Republican who had recently announced his intention to run for the state Senate in the 31st District, asserted that he was gerrymandered into the 33rd District "under cloak of night and pall of secrecy" in the final hours before the Final Plan was adopted, in order to protect the Republican incumbent, Senator John Hopper.[301] A similar claim was raised by Petitioner Lawrence Roberts, who contended that the Commission had drawn him out of the 51st Legislative District to protect the twenty-four-year incumbent, Fred Taylor, after he (Roberts) had moved his home following the Preliminary Plan.[302]

Several petitioners, particularly in Philadelphia, raised claims under the Federal Voting Rights Act. Most significant of these was the petition of Senator F. Joseph Loeper, the Commission member, which asserted that the Final Plan violated the Federal Voting Rights Act because the four minority seats created in Philadelphia fell below the 65% "rule of thumb" required by federal law and because the Final Plan had failed to create a "minority-influenced" or "majority-minority" seat in Pittsburgh.[303]

Sixth, the Petitions of Senator Frank Pecora and Senator F. Joseph Loeper claimed that the collapse of 44th Senate District in Allegheny County, and the transfer of that seat to Chester County, unconstitutionally truncated the term of a duly-elected Senator (i.e. Pecora) and thus deprived the voters of the 44th District an opportunity to elect their own senator.[304]

---

[299] Brief of Respondent, *supra*, at 11; *see also* Petitions for Review of Lawrence Roberts, No. 134 W.D. Pa. Misc. Dkt. (Dec. 12, 1991); Thomas Rabbitt Zajac, No. 135 W.D. Pa. Misc. Dkt. (Dec. 12, 1991); Township of South Union, No. 136 W.D. Misc. Dkt. (Dec. 12, 1991) (State Archives).

[300] Brief of Respondent, *supra*, at 13; *see also* Petition of Dante G. Bertani, No. 141 W.D. Misc. Dkt. (Dec. 13, 1991) (State Archives).

[301] Brief of Respondent, *supra*, at 15; *see also* Petition of Clifford L. Jones, No. 51 M.D. Misc. Dkt. (Dec. 13, 1991) (State Archives).

[302] *See* Petition of Lawrence Roberts, *supra*. Lawrence averred that an unnamed Commission member sought to persuade him to strike a deal with Representative Taylor in exchange for an agreement not to run. When he refused, Roberts averred that the Commission member stated: "Then understand we'll do whatever is necessary to protect Taylor's position." *Id.* at 3.

[303] Brief of Respondent, *supra*, at 27. The proposed Loeper plan in Philadelphia would have had the incidental effect of creating a more attractive seat for Republicans in the 2nd Senate District. The proposed Loeper plan in Pittsburgh would have had the incidental effect of preserving the seat of incumbent Senator Frank Pecora, whose district was collapsed and moved east.

[304] Brief of Respondent, *supra*, at 34-39.

Finally, a scattered number of petitioners urged that they should be entitled to depose and/or take discovery with respect to Commission members and their staffs concerning their motivations, purposes, and thought processes in adopting the Final Plan, in order to flush out further evidence of alleged constitutional violations.[305]

C. Two Dozen Oral Arguments

The night before oral argument, Counsel for the Commission sat up past midnight in a room covered with maps to digest facts and prepare for questions on twenty-three separate cases.[306] Shortly after 9:00 a.m. the following morning, a long line of petitioners proceeded to the podium one by one and briefly presented their cases. Chief Counsel Harmelin rose in a packed courtroom and addressed six of the seven Justices of the Pennsylvania Supreme Court, methodically moving through the dozen petitions that had raised compactness problems and improper "splits" of political boundaries. Associate Counsel Laurence Shtasel, a graduate of Harvard Law School and former Associate Counsel to the Special Prosecutor in the Iran-Contra affair, handled those petitions dealing with the Voting Rights Act challenges. Associate Counsel Barbara Brown Krancer, a *Phi Beta Kappa* graduate of Oberlin College and Moot Court Board member at George Washington University National Law Center, addressed those petitions involving alleged political gerrymandering and the knotty issues regarding Senator Pecora.

In its questioning, the Court indicated particular concern with certain "last minute" changes to the Final Plan, such as those involving Clifford Jones and Lawrence Roberts, which seemed to reflect political mischief. Although the Court did not agree with petitioners' suggestions that they possessed a "right" to run in a particular district, the Court nonetheless appeared troubled that final-hour changes were made in the preliminary map without any realistic opportunity for public comment. The Court also seemed concerned with a number of "splits" of municipal boundaries, including the seven-way split in Westmoreland County. Several Justices pressed both the Commission attorneys and petitioners in an apparent effort to determine whether minor revisions to the map might be made by the Court to correct obvious injustices, without triggering a "domino effect" and upsetting the Plan across the rest of Pennsylvania.

As to Senator Pecora's contention that he had been unconstitutionally deprived of his seat, the Court appeared unpersuaded. Several Justices suggested that Senator Pecora could simply serve out his term in the new 44th District in Chester County, thus vitiating his argument that he had "lost" his seat.

On the voting rights questions, however, the Court appeared most interested and alert, questioning attorney David Norcross vigorously with respect to the Republican Party's contention that the four newly-created minority senate seats in Philadelphia fell below the mandate of the federal act.

D. The Supreme Court Upholds the Plan

At the request of the Court, the Commission filed several supplemental briefs following oral argument to assist the Justices in digesting the complex issues regarding the Voting Rights Act, the timing of circulating nominating petitions for

---

[305] *Id.* at 42.
[306] Two of the twenty-five petitions filed were submitted on the briefs.

the next election, and residency requirements for legislators who were displaced by reapportionment and wished to run in their new districts.[307] Cognizant of the need to reach a prompt decision to avoid disrupting primary elections (lead time is required in order for candidates to circulate petitions, the Secretary of the Commonwealth to certify ballots, and challengers to seek redress in courts if signatures on petitions are claimed invalid), the Pennsylvania Supreme Court issued a brief order upholding the Final Plan on February 14, 1992. The Court, in a three-paragraph *per curiam* opinion, wrote simply that the Final Plan "is not contrary to law" and denied all twenty-five petitions challenging the Final Plan. A written opinion explaining the reasoning of the Court would follow at a later date. In the meantime, elections would move forward.

It was not until May 1, 1992, that Chief Justice Robert N.C. Nix, Jr., the first African-American Justice to preside over the Pennsylvania Supreme Court, issued a full opinion in the reapportionment cases. There was no dissent.[308] Chief Justice Nix began by underscoring that the Constitution clearly stated, and the Court had previously held, that "to prevail in their challenge to the final reapportionment plan, appellants have the burden of establishing not ... that there exists an alternative plan which is 'preferable' or 'better,' but rather that the final plan filed by the Pennsylvania Reapportionment Commission fails to meet constitutional requirements."[309] Chief Justice Nix went on to address each cluster of petitions and found that none had demonstrated that the Final Plan adopted by the Commission was unconstitutional or contrary to law.

Re-embracing, first, the principle that "the overriding objective of reapportionment is equality of population,"[310] the Court noted with approval that the 1991 Reapportionment Plan "compares favorably" with the 1981 and 1971 plans, with a "total percentage deviation from [the] ideal district population" of 1.87% in the Senate and 4.94% in the House.[311] Given the overriding concern of one-person-one-vote, the Court found it inevitable that certain political boundaries would be split and that certain incumbent senators and representatives would be displaced.[312]

The Court also categorically rejected the claim of Senator Pecora and others that the merger of the 43rd and 44th Senatorial Districts in Allegheny County was unconstitutional because the merger upset the system of "staggered elections" in Pennsylvania, thus truncating a Senator's term and assigning him to a wholly

---

[307] *See, e.g.*, Respondent Pennsylvania Legislative Reapportionment Commission's Memorandum of Law on the Effective Date of the Final Reapportionment Plan (Jan. 29, 1992) (State Archives); Letter to Prothonotary (Jan. 29, 1992) (re: "Minority Influence" Plan in Allegheny County) (State Archives).

[308] *See In re* 1991 Pennsylvania Legislative Reapportionment Comm'n, 530 Pa. 335, 609 A.2d 132 (1992), *cert. denied sub nom.* Loeper v. Pennsylvania Reapportionment Comm'n, 113 S. Ct. 66 (1992). Justice Larsen did not participate at oral argument, nor in the decision of the cases. Justices Flaherty and Papadakos did not participate in consideration or decisions with respect to those eight petitions which were heard in the afternoon of oral argument, since they left the oral argument at noon due to other commitments.

[309] *Id.* at 343, 609 A.2d at 136 (quoting *In re* Reapportionment Plan for Pennsylvania General Assembly, 497 Pa. 525, 532, 442 A.2d 661, 665 (1981)). *See also* Gaffney v. Cummings, 412 U.S. 735, 750-51 (1973).

[310] *In re* 1991 Pennsylvania Legislative Reapportionment Commission, 530 Pa. at 349, 609 A.2d at 138-39, *citing* Reynolds v. Sims, 377 U.S. 533, 579 (1964).

[311] *Id.* at 348, 442 A.2d at 138. The corresponding percentages in 1981 were 1.93% (Senate) and 2.81% (House). In 1971 they were 4.31% (Senate) and 5.45% (House).

[312] *Id.*

new constituency that had not elected him. The Pennsylvania Constitution, wrote the Court, "does not include a requirement that all senatorial districts be redrawn in such a manner that incumbent senators remain residents of their redrawn districts."[313] Moreover, the Court noted that Senator Pecora was not automatically expelled from his Senate seat, even after the 44th District had moved east. "Only the Senate," explained the Court, "has the authority to judge the qualifications of its members."[314] Nor was Senator Pecora deprived of a constitutionally protected interest. An elected official's interest in his or her office was "highly circumscribed" and did not merit constitutional job protection.[315] Finally, the citizens of the new 44th District lacked a colorable claim. If the Senate did not seat Senator Pecora as the rightful heir to the new seat, "the citizens of the district will be represented in the Senate by operation of the special election statute."[316]

Turning to those petitions which charged the Commission with unlawful political gerrymandering, the Court reviewed the teachings of the U.S. Supreme Court in *Davis v. Bandemer*[317] and concluded that no such constitutional violation had been established. Even when considering the most extreme cases of Clifford Jones and Lawrence Roberts, there was "no precedent in this state nor in the federal courts for a claim arising from the deprivation of an individual's right to run for a particular office nor of a citizens' right to vote for a specific individual."[318] Absent any evidence of petitioners belonging to "an identifiable group suffering a history of disenfranchisement or lack of political power," a *Bandemer* claim necessarily failed.[319]

The Court also found no merit in the petitions alleging Federal Voting Rights Act violations. The Chief Justice noted that Senator Loeper and the other petitioners were not bringing an action for relief *per se* under the Voting Rights Act. Senator Loeper was not a member of a minority group and thus lacked standing; moreover, the Voting Rights Act specifically provided that the "proper forum" to prosecute such claims was the federal district court.[320] Petitioners were at best asserting that the proposed reapportionment plan was "contrary to law" because it did not conform with the federal act,[321] rather than launching a direct claim under the Voting Rights Act.

Moreover, the Court found no support for petitioners' contention. The Court held that it was irrelevant whether petitioners could supply different maps which provided alternative or even better ways to create minority districts. The sole question was whether the Final Plan as adopted was "contrary to law." Here, although the four majority-minority Senate seats created by the Commission in Philadelphia did not meet the 65% rule of thumb, "[t]here is no requirement under federal law for a 60% to 65% minority population."[322] Indeed, Chief Justice Nix pointed out that the U.S. Supreme Court and other courts had approved various plans

---

[313] *Id.* at 352, 609 A.2d at 140.

[314] *Id.*

[315] *Id.* at 353, 609 A.2d at 140-41.

[316] *Id.* at 354, 609 A.2d at 141. The special election statute is codified at 25 PA. CONS. STAT. ANN. §2778.

[317] 478 U.S. 109 (1986).

[318] *In re* 1991 Pennsylvania Legislative Reapportionment Commission, 530 Pa. at 356, 609 A.2d at 142.

[319] *Id.*

[320] *Id.* at 358 & n.10, 609 A.2d at 143 & n.10.

[321] *Id.*

[322] *Id.* at 363, 609 A.2d at 145-46.

which fell below the 65% "magic number," recognizing that the ultimate goal was simply to ensure that minorities were able to elect candidates of choice.

The Final Plan fashioned by the Commission established an additional minority Senate seat in Philadelphia by creating a configuration in the 3rd Senate District which contained an African-American population of 60.63% and an African-American voting age population of 58%. The 4th Senate District contained a 61.52% African-American population and an African-American voting age population of 58%. The 7th Senate District contained an African-American population of 61.81% and an African-American voting age population of 58%. The 8th Senate District contained an African-American population of 60.14% and an African-American voting age population of 56%. Not only did the Court conclude that this array of minority percentages "clearly fits within the intent of the Voting Rights Act," but the Court further declared that "the plan adopted by the Commission provides for the optimum distribution of the black population in a manner that would support electing or influencing additional representatives of their choice."[323]

Chief Justice Nix also noted that none of the incumbent African-American Senators in the 3rd, 7th, or 8th Senatorial Districts had joined in the attack upon the Commission's plan, "nor have they evinced in any way their concurrence in the alleged concerns."[324]

Finally, the Court rejected the claim of Petitioner Loeper that the Commission had failed to create a "minority influenced seat" in Pittsburgh, which would have (incidentally) saved Senator Pecora's seat. The Court suggested that it was unclear whether such an "influence" seat was constitutionally or statutorily required.[325] The Court noted with approval that the Commission had created a 38th Senatorial District in Allegheny County containing 34% African-American population, which seemed to be sufficient to "provide the minority an opportunity to influence the outcome of elections."[326]

Thus, the Court upheld the 1991 Plan of Reapportionment in all respects. The Court also noted that the Plan had become effective on February 14, 1992, the day the Court issued its original order dismissing the appeals.[327] A number of petitioners sought rearguments or clarifications; the Court denied these petitions within weeks. Senator Pecora, Senator Loeper, and several other challengers promptly filed petitions for writs of certiorari to the United States Supreme Court.[328] On October 5, 1992, the United States Supreme Court denied certiorari, ending an appeals process that had spanned nearly one full year.[329]

---

[323] *Id.* at 364, 609 A.2d at 146.

[324] *Id.* at 362 n.14, 609 A.2d at 145 n.14.

[325] *Id.* at 364-65, 609 A.2d at 146-47. The Court distinguished the recent decision of a three-judge District Court panel in Armour v. Ohio, 775 F. Supp. 1044 (N.D. Ohio 1991), noting that case involved a finding of *intentional* discrimination designed to thwart the Voting Rights Act, the Fifteenth Amendment to the U.S. Constitution, and the Constitution of Ohio.

[326] *Id.* at 365 n.18, 609 A.2d at 147 n.18.

[327] *Id.* at 350, 609 A.2d at 139. Several petitioners had argued that the effective date of the Final Plan should be *after* the November elections to avoid difficulties with the residency requirement, particularly for legislators whose seats were displaced or moved during the reapportionment process. The Court declined this invitation, but noted that the residency requirements might have to be waived or become more flexible during reapportionment years. *Id.* at 350 n.7, 609 A.2d at 139 n.7. The Court would address this issue if and when it became ripe.

[328] To avoid adding to the mounting costs of litigation, the Commission entered a *pro forma* appearance but did not file a formal reply to those petitions.

[329] *See* Loeper v. Pennsylvania Legislative Reapportionment Comm'n, 113 S. Ct. 66 (1992).

XI.
THE PHILADELPHIA VOTING RIGHTS SUIT

A. A Suit is Filed in Federal Court

Five days after oral argument before the Pennsylvania Supreme Court, six minority voters from the City of Philadelphia filed a federal lawsuit against the Commission in the United States District Court for the Eastern District of Pennsylvania. In a case captioned *William M. Harrison et al. v. Pennsylvania Legislative Reapportionment Commission*, filed on January 30, 1992,[330] the plaintiffs alleged a violation of the Voting Rights Act of 1965 and sought a preliminary and permanent injunction to block implementation of the new reapportionment plan as it applied to the state Senate. The plaintiffs claimed that the Final Plan had failed to create 65% minority districts and therefore violated the Voting Rights Act. Represented by Louis W. Fryman and David B. Snyder of the Fox Rothschild firm in Philadelphia, the *Harrison* plaintiffs filed a brief outlining the standards set forth by the U.S. Supreme Court in *Thornburg v. Gingles* and contended that the plaintiffs would demonstrate at the time of hearing "that *none* of the proposed districts (in the Philadelphia Senate map) meet this standard."[331] Plaintiffs went on to argue that a strong public interest existed in favor of enjoining implementation of the new Final Plan because it rendered countless minority citizens' right to vote impotent. The plaintiffs concluded that the court should grant an injunction because the minority plaintiffs would suffer "immediate, irreparable harm" if immediate relief was not granted.[332]

The Commission filed a brief motion requesting that the district court abstain until the Pennsylvania Supreme Court acted on the Voting Rights Act claim already pending in state court.[333] By agreement of counsel, U.S. District Judge John P. Fullam, to whom the case had been assigned, transferred the case to the "suspense docket" pending a decision by the Pennsylvania Supreme Court.[334] Following the *per curiam* decision of the Pennsylvania Supreme Court upholding the plan in mid-February, however, Judge Fullam removed the case from the suspense docket, consolidated the hearing on the motion for preliminary injunction with a trial on the merits, and scheduled a trial for April 2, 1992.

Formal discovery was sharply limited to depositions of the six named plaintiffs, as well as interrogatories and depositions flushing out the theories of the two competing experts. The Commission again retained the services of Dr. Richard L. Engstrom, the Voting Rights Act expert who had advised the Commission's legal counsel throughout the reapportionment process. Plaintiffs hired Dr. Eugene P. Ericksen, a nationally-prominent statistician and sociologist who had extensive background in statistical studies, including some dealing with minority and census issues in Philadelphia, but who had no experience in Voting Rights Act analysis.[335]

---

[330] Civil Action No. 92-CV-0603 (E.D. Pa. Jan. 30, 1992) (State Archives). Brenda K. Mitchell, Acting Secretary of the Commonwealth, was also a nominal defendant.

[331] Memorandum of Law in Support of Motion for a Preliminary Injunction 12 (Jan. 30, 1992) (State Archives).

[332] *Id.* at 17-18.

[333] Defendant Pennsylvania Legislative Reapportionment Commission's Motion to Dismiss and to Abstain a Response to Plaintiffs' Motion for Preliminary Injunction (Feb. 3, 1992) (State Archives).

[334] *See* Order Civil Action No. 92-603 (Feb. 7, 1992) (State Archives).

[335] *See* Plaintiffs' Response to Pennsylvania Legislative Reapportionment Commission's first set of interrogatories and attached *curriculum vitae* of Eugene P. Ericksen (Mar. 13, 1992) (State Archives).

A number of developments prior to trial became significant. The Commission's counsel, in conducting depositions of the six named plaintiffs, discovered that these individuals had very little independent knowledge regarding the lawsuit. The Commission's counsel determined that all six plaintiffs had been recruited by the Republican City Committee of Philadelphia to serve as challengers to the Final Plan. Thus, the Commission was able to obtain a written stipulation that all of the plaintiffs, four of whom were African-American and two of whom were Hispanic, had been recruited by Joseph Duda, Executive Director of the Republican City Committee, based upon a concern that the Final Plan "may be in violation of the applicable law and that it did not create adequate opportunities for Republican candidates to win elections in Philadelphia's seven senatorial districts."[336] More-over, the stipulation stated that all fees and costs of the litigation were being covered by the Republican City Committee, not the individual plaintiffs.[337] This stipulation was significant because it alerted the trial judge to the fact that partisan interests were at work rather than a grass roots campaign of racial minorities. Indeed, a separate stipulation of counsel acknowledged that none of the minority groups who had actively provided comment during the reapportionment process had challenged the Final Plan.[338]

Second, the differences between the expert opinions quickly manifested themselves, making the legal issues fairly clear-cut. The crux of Dr. Engstrom's argument, on behalf of the Commission, was that the four majority-minority senate seats created by the Final Plan comfortably satisfied the *Gingles* requirements. The existing minority senatorial seats *prior* to the 1991 Final Plan looked like this:

District	African-American Population	Latino Population
3rd	85.3%	7.7%
7th	70.0%	1.3%
8th	64.3%	.1%

Under the Final Plan adopted by the Commission, the four new majority-minority seats could be broken down as follows:[339]

District	African-American Population	Latino Population	African-American Voting Age Population
3rd	60.63%	.5%	58.3%
4th	61.52%	1.1%	58.7%
7th	61.81%	1.1%	58.1%
8th	60.14%	1.2%	56.8%

Additionally, the 2nd District under the Final Plan contained a Latino population of approximately 23%, with the bulk of the remaining population white.

Dr. Engstrom analyzed a host of general and primary election results, primarily at the precinct level in Philadelphia. These included results of presidential, con-

---

[336] *See* Defendant Pennsylvania Legislative Reapportionment Commission's Pre-Hearing Statement, Pre-Hearing Memorandum of Law and Proposed Findings of Fact and Conclusions of Law, Exhibit C (Apr. 1, 1992) (State Archives).

[337] *Id.*

[338] *Id.* at Exhibit A.

[339] *See id.* at Exhibit A.

gressional, gubernatorial, mayoral, senatorial, legislative, and local races. Dr. Engstrom obtained data from the LDPC, the Philadelphia Commissioner's Office, the Montgomery County Board of Elections, and other sources.[340] By performing regression analyses, simulating new elections, and conducting reaggregation studies to "rerun" past elections in the new districts,[341] Professor Engstrom reached several important conclusions. First, he determined that the African-American community in Philadelphia was politically cohesive. Second, African-American voters in Philadelphia had, surprisingly, a very high voter turnout in primary elections — indeed, higher than whites. Third, there was a substantial "crossover voting" by white voters for African-American candidates in general elections in Philadelphia; in other words, white citizens often voted for the African-American candidate rather than competing white candidates. Fourth, in state legislative elections in Philadelphia, white voters did not consistently defeat minority candidates by bloc voting. Fifth, evidence gathered in Philadelphia did *not* show that Latinos and African-Americans voted cohesively.[342]

Based upon the high levels of African-American voter turnout and white crossover voting, Dr. Engstrom concluded that the percentage of minority population in the four majority-minority districts *did not need to reach 65%* in order to provide African-American voters with a reasonable opportunity to elect candidates of choice. Indeed, the voting age populations of African-Americans was high enough to comfortably elect African-Americans in all four districts the Commission had built. Of equal significance, Dr. Engstrom concluded that there were marked problems with "aggregating" or combining African-Americans and Latinos into a single district to reach higher "minority" totals. African-Americans and Latinos, according to his analysis, did not consistently vote together in Philadelphia.[343]

In contrast, plaintiffs' expert, Dr. Ericksen, took the position that the four minority senate seats created by the Commission were insufficient to elect minority candidates. Due to a history of white bloc voting, as well as differences between the minority community and white community in factors such as age, voter registration, and voter turnouts, Dr. Ericksen concluded that absent a 65% minority population, the white majority would usually be able to defeat a minority candidate.[344] On the other hand, he believed that the African-American and Hispanic communities were "sufficiently able and geographically compact to constitute a majority in a single member district" and that the two groups voted "cohesively."[345]

The plaintiffs therefore contended that the only way to build four "legitimate" majority-minority seats was to aggregate the African-American and Latino voters into a single district (the 3rd Senatorial District) to create a fourth minority district. Although plaintiffs proposed no specific plan in this regard, a similar proposal by Senator Loeper during the reapportionment process would have yielded

---

[340] *Id.* at Exhibit B.

[341] For a discussion of these three methodologies, which are common to Voting Rights Act analyses, *see* The Pennsylvania Legislative Reapportionment Commission's Post-Hearing Brief (Apr. 13, 1992) (State Archives) and attached exhibits.

[342] *See* Defendant's Pre-Hearing Statement, *supra*, at 13-15; *see also* Post-Hearing Brief, *supra*, Defendant's Exhibits 6-19.

[343] Defendant's Pre-Hearing Statement, *supra*, at 13-16.

[344] *See* Plaintiffs' Trial Brief 4-5 (Apr. 1, 1992) (State Archives).

[345] *Id.* at 14-15.

districts including one "aggregated" district containing 25.6% Latino voters and 54.9% African-American voters. Such a revised map of Philadelphia would have yielded the following four majority-minority districts:[346]

District	Black Population	Latino Population	Total Minority Population
3rd	54.9%	25.6%	80.5%
4th	65.0%	—	65.0%
7th	65.8%	—	65.8%
8th	66.5%	—	66.5%

Thus, the battle lines were sharply drawn between the two experts. Much of the evidence was submitted by stipulation between the parties.

As the trial grew closer, the Commission faced several unusual (and awkward) situations. First, the Commission was required to argue to Judge Fullam that the Commission itself was not the proper party to the suit but that it nonetheless wished to argue the case as *amicus curiae*.[347] This unusual turn of events was necessitated by Counsel's conclusion that the Commission possessed legislative immunity from suit and therefore was not the proper defendant. At the same time, Counsel for the Commission was clearly the ideal attorney to handle this litigation. Requiring the Office of General Counsel, who represented the Governor and Secretary of the Commonwealth, to become actively involved at the tail end of the lengthy reapportionment battle would have represented a disservice to the voting public, who had an interest in the matter being intelligently and cost-effectively resolved. Thus, it made sense for the Commission to remain involved and to supervise the trial as *amicus curiae*. A similar approach had been sanctioned by other courts in previous reapportionment matters.[348] In the end, Judge Fullam decided the matter by inaction, allowing the Commission to preserve its "immunity" defense but never directly ruling on the issue. Based upon this somewhat tenuous footing, the Commission moved forward and prepared for trial.

The second awkward situation faced by the Commission was that it was required to deal with one Commission member as both a colleague and an adversary. Republican Senator F. Joseph Loeper, a member of the Commission, had openly opposed the Final Plan on a number of grounds, including the configuration of the minority senate districts in Philadelphia. Having explicitly challenged the Final Plan in the Pennsylvania Supreme Court, Senator Loeper was unabashedly sympathetic with the plaintiffs' position in the *Harrison* litigation; indeed, the Republican City Committee of Philadelphia had taken an active role in recruiting the plaintiffs and paying for the expert witness, as stipulated by the attorneys. Thus, Commission's counsel was in the difficult position of having to deal with Senator Loeper and his staff *qua* Commission member, on one hand, and, on the other hand, having to construct a "Chinese wall" around him to avoid revealing infor-

---

[346] *See* Defendant's Pre-Hearing Statement, *supra*, at Exhibit B; *see also* Transcript of Legislative Reapportionment Commission Public Meeting 20-21 (Nov. 15, 1991) (State Archives).

[347] *See* Pennsylvania Legislative Reapportionment Commission's Motion to Dismiss and for Leave to Appear as Amicus Curiae (Apr. 1, 1992) (State Archives).

[348] *Id.* at 2-3. *See* Pennsylvania Environment Defense Found. v. Bellefonte Borough, 718 F. Supp. 431, 434-35 (M.D. Pa. 1989); Jones v. Pennsylvania Legislative Reapportionment Comm'n, No. 4: CV-92-0279 (M.D. Pa. 1992).

mation which might have an adverse impact upon the Commission's trial preparation.

Commission's counsel dealt with this situation in the same fashion that an attorney representing a corporation might deal with adversarial relationships among board members or officers. The "client" was the Commission itself. Where potential conflicts were perceived to exist in dealing with either political party, or either caucus, the Commission's counsel took guidance from the Chairman and Executive Director, as the neutral representatives of the body, to formulate trial strategy untainted by adversarial relationships.

B. The Trial (Judge Fullam)

On April 2, 1992, the Honorable John P. Fullam, Senior Judge of the United States District Court for the Eastern District of Pennsylvania, conducted a tightly-controlled trial on the Federal Voting Rights Act claim. Much of the evidence was presented by stipulation of the lawyers. The named plaintiffs never took the stand. Plaintiffs' entire case, in essence, rested on the testimony of Professor Eugene Ericksen, who opined that the four minority districts created by the Commission would not allow minorities to elect candidates of choice. Once again, Professor Ericksen took the position (favored by the Republican party) that the minority population percentages should be increased by combining Latino and African-American voters into the 3rd District, thus allowing minority percentages to rise in the other three districts.

The Commission's case, handled by litigation counsel Lawrence Shtasel and Barbara Brown Krancer from the Dilworth firm (along with Martin Bryce, an Order of the Coif graduate of Villanova Law School, on the briefs) focussed on the live testimony of Professor Richard L. Engstrom. In great detail, Professor Engstrom moved through his voting rights analysis and explained that the four minority seats created by the Commission were more than adequate to allow minorities to elect candidates of choice. Dr. Engstrom had analyzed nearly all primary and general elections in the Philadelphia area over the past six years in which biracial slates of candidates had been presented to voters. Based upon this data, Professor Engstrom concluded that (1) African-Americans in Philadelphia exhibited polarized voting, that is, they tended to vote for African-American voters when presented with a biracial slate; (2) African-Americans tended to vote in primary elections at rates higher than whites, allowing them to influence primary elections in a significant fashion; and (3) general elections were marked by a strong white crossover vote for African-American Democratic candidates even when a biracial slate was presented, meaning that white voters tended to add support to the black candidates in the general election.[349] Based upon these three findings, Professor Engstrom strongly concluded that districts containing approximately 61% African-American voters would have a reasonable opportunity, indeed a comfortable likelihood, of nominating and electing candidates of the minority group's own choice.

As Professor Engstrom explained, the original 65% rule of thumb (which was developed largely in southern states with a strong history of discrimination), added

---

[349] For a more in-depth discussion of Professor Engstrom's analysis, see Pennsylvania Legislative Reappportionment Commission's Post-Hearing Brief 5-15 (Apr. 13, 1992) (State Archives). See also id. at 6-19 (attached to document as Exhibit A).

15% to a traditional 50% "majority" by taking into account three factors: (a) a 5% adjustment for low voter turnout among minorities; (b) a 5% adjustment for low white crossover voting for minority candidates; and (c) a 5% adjustment for the relatively young population of minorities.[350] Based upon his analysis of election results in Philadelphia, not to mention the fact that Philadelphia already had a long history of black political incumbency, Professor Engstrom concluded that 65% minority population districts were "simply unnecessary in Philadelphia to ensure that the resident minority voters in the districts are afforded an equal opportunity to participate in the political process and to elect representatives of their choice."[351]

Of equal importance, Professor Engstrom stressed that the plaintiffs' proposal for combining African-Americans and Latinos into a single "aggregate" district was dangerously flawed. First, it resulted in minority districts well in excess of 70% minority population that could be challenged under the Voting Rights Act as being "packed."[352] Second, the plaintiffs' proposal, which virtually mirrored the Republican proposal throughout the reapportionment process, presumed that African-Americans and Latinos voted cohesively, which Engstrom's analysis did not support. Moreover, plaintiffs' proposal split the Latino growth area between two districts, rather than placing the entire growth area in a single district as reflected by the Final Plan.[353]

In support of Professor Engstrom's position, Commission's counsel called Patricia DeCarlo, Co-chair of the Philadelphia Latino Voting Rights Committee, who testified concerning the Latino community's active participation in the Commission's reapportionment process. Ms. DeCarlo explained that the Commission had explicitly responded to the Latino community's proposals in both the House and the Senate. In the Senate, the Latino community wished to remain in a single district that corresponded to its natural area of growth, i.e. north and east of Broad Street (the 2nd District),[354] a request which had been embodied in the Final Plan.

Representative Vincent Hughes (D., Philadelphia), Chairman of the Pennsylvania Legislative Black Caucus also testified at trial. Hughes emphasized that the Commission's Final Plan increased the opportunity for African-American voters to elect state senators in Philadelphia,[355] "a positive accomplishment," in his words.

In less than one day, Judge Fullam completed testimony based upon sharp questioning and a mound of stipulated evidence. Thus concluded the Federal Voting Rights Act trial.

C. The Commission Prevails

On April 21, 1992, Judge Fullam issued a brief, seven-page opinion and order, concluding that the Final Plan did not violate the Federal Voting Rights Act.[356] In a

---

[350] *Id.* at 12.
[351] *Id.*
[352] "Packing" refers to the dilution of a minority's political efficacy by placing so many minority voters in a single district that their votes are "wasted" elsewhere. Indeed, one result of the plaintiffs' plan was that it virtually eliminated minority voters from the 2nd Senate District, and increased the chances of a Republican being elected in that district.
[353] Post Hearing Brief at 15.
[354] *Id.* at 11.
[355] *Id.* at 10-11.
[356] *See* Harrison v. Pennsylvania Legislative Reapportionment Comm'n, 1992 U.S. Dist. LEXIS 5313 (E.D. Pa. Apr. 21, 1992).

nutshell, Judge Fullam found the Commission's expert testimony to be persuasive and agreed that the four new minority senate seats created in Philadelphia were a step forward for African-American and Latino citizens in those districts.

Judge Fullam began by observing that the U.S. Supreme Court in *Thornburg v. Gingles* had set out a number of factors to determine whether a districting plan violated Section 2 of the Voting Rights Act. These factors included (1) the extent to which there existed any history of official discrimination in the state or political subdivision, (2) the extent to which voting was racially polarized, (3) the extent to which the state or political subdivision had used unusually large election districts, majority vote requirements, anti-single-shot provisions, or other voting practices or procedures that increased the opportunity for discrimination against minorities, (4) whether minorities had access to the candidate slating process, and (5) the extent to which members of the minority group had been adversely affected by past discrimination in ways which would hinder their ability to participate effectively in the political process.[357]

In the case before him, Judge Fullam noted that the parties had focussed almost exclusively upon the second factor, namely the impact of bloc voting along racial lines. As the Supreme Court had instructed in *Gingles*:

> The purpose of inquiring into the existence of racially polarized voting is twofold: to ascertain whether minority group members constitute a politically cohesive unit and to determine whether whites vote sufficiently as a bloc usually to defeat the minority's preferred candidates ....[358]

Judge Fullam concluded that the Commission's evidence, including the persuasive testimony of Professor Engstrom, "clearly establishes that, in each of the state senatorial districts under challenge, the percentage of African-Americans is sufficient to assure that they can both nominate and elect candidates of their choice."[359]

Indeed, the court concluded that plaintiffs' own expert testimony led to the same conclusion. Dr. Ericksen's numbers revealed that African-American voters tended to vote cohesively and that there was a substantial percentage of white crossover voting for African-American candidates in Philadelphia. Given this uncontroverted data, the 65% rule of thumb could not be viewed as "a hard and fast rule." The Commission's Final Plan safely created four senatorial districts which satisfied the *Gingles* criteria. Indeed, Judge Fullam found it significant that the Final Plan "has the unanimous support of all minority organizations" who actively participated in the reapportionment process. Furthermore, Judge Fullam appeared concerned that the plaintiffs' proposal, identical to the plan proposed by Senate Republicans, would create districts with extremely high minority populations. In Judge Fullam's words, this was "likely to constitute improper 'packing' — *i.e.*, relegating minority voters to electing a single representative, and giving white voters a likely monopoly in other districts."[360]

On the basis of the evidence viewed as a whole, Judge Fullam was satisfied that the *Harrison* plaintiffs had failed to demonstrate that the Commission's Final Plan violated Section 2 of the Voting Rights Act. The suit was dismissed, and plaintiffs elected not to pursue any further appeal.

---

[357] *Id.* at *3.
[358] *Id.* at *4-5, quoting Thornburg v. Gingles, 478 U.S. at 56.
[359] *Id.* at *5.
[360] *Id.*

XII.
SENATOR PECORA AND
THE CHESTER COUNTY SUIT

In the waning days of 1992, just as the Commission was preparing to balance its budget and close up its operations, another major suit was filed in federal court, this one in some ways more ominous than the last. The suit was brought by a group of voters in Chester, Montgomery, Berks, and Lehigh Counties, challenging the right of Senator Frank Pecora to continue to represent the new 44th District after its transplantation to the eastern part of the state. What made this suit more disturbing than those that had preceded it was that this suit was fashioned under the Federal Civil Rights Act, naming the Chairman and individual Commission members, personally, as defendants. Additionally, this suit raised the immediate prospect of taking depositions of Commission members and their staffs in an attempt to pierce the legislative immunity that had thus far been preserved.

The Chester County suit traced its way back to the stormy collapse of Senator Pecora's seat in western Pennsylvania and the reemergence of his 44th District seat in eastern Pennsylvania. The colorful, cigar-chomping Pecora had waged an unsuccessful battle in the Pennsylvania Supreme Court, challenging the decision of the Commission to eliminate his seat.[361] This avenue having failed, Pecora then pursued a series of roller coaster-like political maneuvers which left his own political party stunned and the voters of the new 44th District incensed.

Pecora first switched his party registration and became a Democrat, in March of 1992, throwing his hat into the ring for the Democratic primary in the newly-drawn 18th U.S. Congressional District, a heavily Democratic piece of turf.[362] This left Senate Republicans in Harrisburg nonplussed and uneasy. The Republican majority in the Senate had been reduced to 26-to-24 in 1990, meaning that a single defection to the Democrats would create a 25-to-25 split. Pecora had once before switched parties from Democrat to Republican prior to becoming a state Senator and had openly wooed Democrats in 1990, reportedly offering to switch sides of the aisle in return for the position of President Pro Tempore of the Senate, a deal that never materialized. Republicans feared the worst if Pecora chose to take a seat on the Democratic side of the Chamber after the election played out.[363]

After winning the April Democratic primary for the U.S. Congressional seat in a busy field of candidates, Pecora surprised political observers of both parties by suffering a resounding defeat in the general election against incumbent Congressman Rick Santorum (R., Mount Lebanon), who won by a hefty margin in a district that was approximately 70% Democratic.[364] Following this loss in November of 1992, Pecora reported to his usual place of work in the Pennsylvania Senate, seeking to be seated as the incumbent Senator from the transplanted 44th District. Despite private conversations in which he had reportedly assured Republicans that he would continue to be seated and vote on the Republican side of the aisle, Pecora

---

[361] *See supra* text accompanying notes 313-16.

[362] *See* Gary Tuma, *Pecora Switches, Becomes a Democrat*, PITT. POST-GAZETTE, Mar. 3, 1992, at 10.

[363] *See* Robert Zausner, *One Little-known Lawmaker Sending Pa. Senate Into a Tizzy*, THE PHILADELPHIA INQUIRER, Sept. 25, 1992, Metro/Part 2 at B9.

[364] Telephone Interview with the Office of the Honorable Rick Santorum, United States House of Representatives (Dec. 10, 1993).

strode into the Senate chamber and voted to elect a Democrat President Pro Tempore.[365]

This produced an uproar in the Senate. After the Senate Democrats defeated moves challenging Pecora as the legitimate Senator representing the newly-transplanted 44th District in southeastern Pennsylvania, a heavily Republican district in which Pecora now rented an apartment, the battle lines for a new lawsuit were drawn.[366]

It was not at all clear that the Reapportionment Commission would be the target of the suit. The Senate of Pennsylvania by law retains the absolute right to determine the legitimacy of its members' credentials.[367] The Lieutenant Governor possesses the sole ability to declare a special election, in the event that a vacancy was deemed to exist in the new 44th District.[368] Thus, it was not clear that the Commission had any power to determine whether Pecora should be seated or removed or to determine if the new 44th District should be declared vacant and a special election held. Nonetheless, the Chester County lawsuit, brought under the caption *Donatelli v. Casey,* named Chairman Cindrich and the other four members of the Commission as individual defendants.[369] The suit, fashioned under the Civil Rights Act of the Reconstruction Era, 42 U.S.C. §1983, alleged that the Commission members, acting under color of state law, had deprived voters in the new 44th District of their equal protection of the laws under the Fourteenth Amendment of the U.S. Constitution. The suit sought, among other things, money damages against Chairman Cindrich, Representative Perzel, and Representative Kukovich personally (the three Commission members who voted in favor of the Final Plan), a court-ordered special election in the new 44th District, and attorney's fees.

The immediate threat posed by the Chester County lawsuit was that the attorneys for defendants Jubelirer and Loeper, who openly sympathized with plaintiffs, quickly issued a subpoena to the Executive Director, seeking to conduct his deposition and have him turn over a plethora of documents and internal notes and memoranda of the Commission. The subpoena requested all letters, correspondence, memoranda, reports, charts, graphs, calendars, and printouts in any way relating

---

[365] *Palace coup: Pecora's revenge shifts majorly,* HARRISBURG PATRIOT NEWS, Nov. 25, 1992. With Senator Pecora's vote, a tie resulted. The Lieutenant Governor's vote broke the tie in favor of the Democrats.

[366] Mark Abrams, *Pecora says he is unshaken by controversy,* READING TIMES, Jan. 6, 1993. An additional vacancy occurred as a result of the resignation of Republican State Senator James C. Greenwood, who had been elected to Congress in the November election. As a result, when the 1993 Senate convened, the Democrats held a 25-24 majority — the first Democrat majority since 1980.

[367] The Pennsylvania Constitution, provides that the Senate is the exclusive "judge of the election and qualifications of its members." PA. CONST. art. II, §9.

[368] *See* PA. CONST. art. II, §2; art. II, §9. *See also* 25 PA. CONS. STAT. ANN. §2778 (Purdon Supp. 1992).

[369] *See* Donatelli v. Casey, 826 F. Supp. 131 (E.D. Pa. 1993). The suit also named as defendants Senator J. William Lincoln (D., Dunbar) and Senator Robert C. Jubelirer (R., Altoona), who had become the new Majority and Minority Leaders of the Senate, respectively, following the realignment of power. The theory of naming these two individuals was that the Pennsylvania Constitution was unclear as to whether the Commission consisted of those party leaders who were initially certified to serve as Commission members, or whether the new party leaders now assumed the status of Commission members. *See* PA. CONST. art. II, §17(b). This issue was later mooted when the putative "new" Commission members simply deputized the existing Commission members to continue to act. It was the clear opinion of the Commission's special counsel, in any event, that the Commission members remained unchanged until the next decennial census, since they had been properly certified. *See* Transcript of Public Meeting 27-30 (Feb. 3, 1993) (State Archives).

to the inner-workings of the Commission.[370] This demand posed a problem because the Commission had long since run out of funds to pay for legal counsel; more seriously, the prospect of turning over such materials, along with depositions, threatened to destroy the legislative immunity that had thus far protected the Commission and its staff. Although Senator Loeper was ostensibly a defendant in the Chester County lawsuit, he clearly shared a common interest with the plaintiffs. The Republican party was anxious to have a special election held in the 44th District, in order to return the balance of power to the Republicans.

The Executive Director therefore filed a *pro se* motion with the federal court in Pittsburgh, seeking to halt his own deposition and quash the subpoena until the Commission had an opportunity to obtain legal counsel to protect its interests. This was critical, the Executive Director argued, to preserve the legislative immunity of the Commission and to protect its rights under the Speech or Debate Clause of the Pennsylvania Constitution.[371] A number of cases in Pennsylvania and elsewhere had suggested that the same legislative immunity that protected legislators and their staffs from lawsuits likewise protected the state Reapportionment Commission.[372] If this were the case, the Speech or Debate Clause of Article II, Section 15, of the Pennsylvania Constitution would clearly safeguard the items belonging to the Commission and its staff requested under the subpoena, just as the Speech or Debate Clause protected the Pennsylvania Legislature itself.[373]

Federal District Judge Gustave Diamond granted the *pro se* motion of the Executive Director, quashing the subpoena and allowing the Commission time to obtain legal counsel to protect its rights as a body. At a hastily convened public meeting held on February 3, 1993, the Commission unanimously approved the hiring of W. Thomas McGough, Jr., as Special Counsel for the Commission. McGough, a highly respected lawyer in Pittsburgh and a former clerk to Justice Rehnquist of the U.S. Supreme Court, had previously handled Section 1983 actions involving public officials and offered to accept the case at a sharply reduced fee to soften the Commission's budgetary problems.

At the insistence of Chairman Cindrich, the Commission made clear that it intended to take no position on the merits of the Chester County action. According to the Chairman, the issue of whether a special election should be called was a purely political issue, over which the Commission had no control and should take no official stance. The sole job of the Special Counsel would be to protect the interests of the *Commission as a body*, as well as the individual members sued for money damages. The primary goal was to ensure that legislative immunity and

---

[370] *See* Subpoena In a Civil Case, Civil Action No. 92-CV-9429 (Jan. 8, 1993) (State Archives).

[371] *See* Pro Se Motion for Protection Order, to Quash Subpoena, and for Stay of Discovery Pending Reasonable Opportunity to Obtain Legal Counsel (E.D. Pa. Civ. No. 92-CV-7429, W.D. Pa. Misc. 93-24 Jan. 21, 1993) (State Archives).

[372] *See, e.g., In re* Reapportionment Plan for Pennsylvania General Assembly, 497 Pa. at 532, 442 A.2d at 665 (holding that the Commission fulfills a legislative function); Lunderstadt v. Colafella, 885 F.2d 66, 73-74 (3d Cir. 1989) (applying federal common law of legislative immunity to Section 1983 actions against state legislators); Hispanic Coalition on Reapportionment v. Legislative Reapportionment Comm'n, 536 F. Supp. 578, 582 n.2 (E.D. Pa. 1982), aff'd, 459 U.S. 801 (1982) (finding that legislative immunity applied to block the deposition of the former Chairman of the Reapportionment Commission); Holmes v. Farmer, 475 A.2d 976, 984 (R.I. 1984) (applying legislative immunity to state reapportionment only).

[373] For a detailed discussion of the legislative immunity and Speech or Debate Clause issues, *see* Brief for Appellees John M. Perzel and Robert J. Cindrich, No. 93-1293 (3d Cir. Apr. 19, 1993) (State Archives).

Speech or Debate Clause guarantees were safeguarded. As far as the fate of Senator Pecora and the proposed Special Election, this could be thrashed out by the Democrats and Republicans in federal court, utilizing their own funds.[374] With the role of the Commission sharply narrowed in this fashion, the Chester County litigation moved forward in an orderly and streamlined fashion, with Special Counsel McGough and his associate Mark Melodia maintaining a low-key role and addressing only the narrow issues that threatened the Commission as an institution.

The case was assigned to Federal Judge Robert S. Gawthrop, III, a former chairman of the Republican Committee of Chester County. Despite his avowed sympathy with the voters of the displaced 44th District, Judge Gawthrop issued an intriguing opinion, after extensive briefing and oral argument, that concluded that no violation of the Federal Civil Rights Act had occurred.[375] Judge Gawthrop first reviewed the law under the Equal Protection Clause of the Fourteenth Amendment and concluded that a "rational basis" test had to be applied. As long as the actions of the Commission in adopting a Final Plan were "rationally related" to a legitimate state interest, they would pass constitutional muster.

Judge Gawthrop first noted with wit and verve that:

> [I]n an apparently unique feat of legislative levitation and legerdemain, the 44th District was whisked 250 miles across the Commonwealth, replete with its own pre-elected senator, and plopped down upon the not entirely unsuspecting, but certainly unelecting, brand new batch of voters in eastern Pennsylvania, as some sort of senatorial manna from the Monogahela.[376]

Judge Gawthrop then acknowledged that there was a clear detriment to the voters of the new 44th District, who would be forced to be represented by Senator Pecora, from the other end of Pennsylvania and for whom none of them had voted, for another two years. In eloquent prose he wrote:

> I do recognize, at first, that there is undeniably a disadvantage visited upon the citizens-plaintiffs in question, that is to say, the voters who now find themselves by quirk of legislative quarrel, firmly ensconced within the remarkably ambulatory 44th Senatorial District. It is true that they did not get to vote for the person who is now their senator. It is true that their senator may have political views that are anathema to them, embracing thoughts diametric to their own. It is true as well that because of the numbering, they are going to be stuck with him as their Senator, all things being equal, until the end of 1994.[377]

Nonetheless, Judge Gawthrop concluded that this "disadvantage" did not rise to the level of a denial of equal protection under the laws. Indeed, he noted that state records indicated that over 1,086,454 other citizens throughout the Commonwealth were being represented by legislators for whom they had not voted following reapportionment.[378] Judge Gawthrop found a "rational basis" for the actions

---

[374] *See* Transcript of the Legislative Reapportionment Commission Public Meeting 8-14 (Feb. 3, 1993) (State Archives).

[375] Donatelli v. Casey, 826 F. Supp. 131 (E.D. Pa. 1993).

[376] *Id.* at 132-33.

[377] *Id.* at 136.

[378] *Id.*

of the Commission in the substantial population shift that had occurred from west to east prior to the 1991 reapportionment. There were a myriad of different ways that the Commission could have handled this dilemma; the Commission chose the approach that moved the 44th District into Chester County. Although other methods may have avoided the specific problem at hand, they may have caused even greater ones. "It is not the function of this court," wrote Judge Gawthrop, "to substitute its judgment and rework that representational jigsaw puzzle, that patchwork quilt of democracy, in a way that better suits the fancy of this writer."[379] Unless the plan was "so perverse, so riddled with irrationality" that one could conclude the Commission lacked a rational basis for its actions, Judge Gawthrop felt duty-bound to uphold the plan.[380]

Thus, Judge Gawthrop upheld the action of the Commission on March 19, 1993, as a "'permissible exercise of its discretion.'"[381] He allowed the new 44th District to stand without ordering a special election.[382] In the meantime, the legislative immunity of the Commission, and its long-term interest as an institution in preserving its rights under the Speech or Debate Clause, remained intact.

The Third Circuit Court of Appeals granted an expedited appeal to the plaintiffs in the Chester County action, allowing the case to be argued and decided in time to permit a special election quickly, if ordered. On July 2, 1993, the case was argued before a three-judge panel of the Third Circuit, with attorneys McGough and Melodia working on the Commission's brief. On August 13th, a unanimous panel affirmed the district court, holding that no violation of the Equal Protection Clause had occurred.

The opinion in *Donatelli v. Mitchell*,[383] authored by Circuit Judge Edward Becker, once again concluded that the proper standard of review was the "highly deferential" rational basis test.[384] Using this standard, the court emphasized that plaintiffs' position was no different than that of over one million other Pennsylvania citizens who were shifted to new districts by virtue of reapportionment and "assigned" a Senator whom they did not elect.[385] Moreover, according to Judge Becker, the contention that the Final Plan ran afoul of Pennsylvania law because it allowed an "appointed" Senator to represent the displaced 44th District rang hollow. The Pennsylvania Supreme Court, the final arbiter of that state's law, had held that Senator Pecora, if seated by the Senate, was the proper representative of the new 44th District for the remaining two years of his term. The Pennsylvania Senate had seated him. Thus, there could be no claim that state law had been subverted.[386] Finally, both federal cases and cases from other states allowed the appointment of unelected individuals to represent districts on an interim basis following reapportionments; Senator Pecora's status was no different.[387]

In the end, the *Donatelli* court concluded that the state had a legitimate interest in avoiding the expense and inconvenience of a special election, as well as a legitimate interest "in not ousting a senator in the middle of the four-year term which he

---

[379] *Id.* at 136.
[380] *Id.*
[381] *Id.*
[382] *Id.*
[383] 2 F.3d 508 (3d Cir. 1993).
[384] *Id.* at 513, 515.
[385] *Id.* at 516.
[386] *Id.* at 517.
[387] *Id.* at 517-18.

was elected to serve.''[388] It could not be said that the state, through the Reapportionment Commission, lacked a rational basis for a Final Plan which inevitably was bound to cause disruption due to massive population shifts beyond its control. Although the Third Circuit was ''not unmindful of the strong intimation in the plaintiffs' papers that political partisanship was a driving force between the unusual chain of events at issue here,'' the court found this to be proof of the adage that federal courts should generally steer clear of political disputes arising out of state reapportionments.[389]

In a footnote, the Third Circuit in *Donatelli* also concluded that it did not need to reach either the issue of the Commission's immunity under the Speech or Debate Clause or of the Commission members' qualified immunity from damages.[390] These issues were, in the end, moot. Thus, the final chapter of the Reapportionment of 1991 was closed, with the Commission able to preserve its rights as a body for the benefit of future Commissions. No decision of any court had indicated that the Commission should receive any less protection than the legislature itself in the face of litigation and political volleying that spilled into the judicial arena.

---

[388] *Id.* at 519.
[389] *Id.*
[390] *Id.* at 519 n.14.

XIII.
RECOMMENDATIONS FOR
FUTURE COMMISSIONS

The experiences of the 1991 Legislative Reapportionment Commission, the most extensive and multifaceted of any reapportionment body in the history of the Commonwealth, provide important lessons for future Commissions both in Pennsylvania and other states. The Chairman and Executive Director, rather than the Commission as a body, offer the following recommendations because no formal action was taken by the Commission in this regard. Although the practicality of politics prevents unamimity on issues of this type, certain general (and hopefully apolitical) recommendations can be offered for future generations of lawyers, citizens and legislators as they grapple with the puzzling challenges of redistricting.

A. Iowa Model versus Pennsylvania Model

Much debate was generated in the press during the 1991 Reapportionment, and within the State Capitol itself, about the virtues of the "Iowa model" for reapportionment.[391] The Iowa model empowers a wholly neutral Commission to randomly create new districts of equal size using a computer program, thus ostensibly eliminating politics from the reapportionment process. The Iowa process has led to nearly 40% of the incumbent representatives being unseated after moving into new districts and having to run against fellow incumbents. Common Cause and other citizens' groups have lauded this approach. The general theory was that the current Pennsylvania system is driven excessively by a desire of incumbents to gain re-election and that politics should be eradicated from the reapportionment process altogether.[392]

There are a number of observations relative to the Iowa model that can be made after the 1991 experience in Pennsylvania. First, clear benefits flow from directly involving the political leaders of the Commonwealth in reapportionment. The political leaders and their staffs know the intricate histories and interests of neighborhoods, towns, regions, and counties across the large expanse of Pennsylvania better than anyone else. Their expertise and talent would be hard, if not impossible, to duplicate in any body comprised of entirely nonpolitical actors and pieced together each ten years. Moreover, party politics tend to balance out naturally; each competing party is quick to point out the problems and inconsistencies created by reapportionment plans presented by the opposing party. Thus, the "politics" of the situation is naturally held in check.

Second, it is far from clear that the Iowa model recommends itself to a state with a widely varied geography like Pennsylvania. Simple computer-generated squares do not work neatly in a state defined by mountains, valleys and twisting riverbanks; farmlands, sprawling urban areas, and imprecise school districts; and 200-year old communities of interest. There are advantages to preserving a continuity in districts, office locations, and, at least to the extent citizens wish, their elected officials. The current Pennsylvania system allows experience and human

---

[391] Don Wolfe, *Iowa hailed as model of redistricting without politics*, PITT. PRESS, Nov. 10, 1991, at B1.
[392] *Id.*

thought to guide the pen of reapportionment, rather than random computer-driven hash marks. This is a considerable benefit, ultimately, to citizens who wish to live in representative districts defined loosely by true communities of interest.

Finally, when the framers drafted the reapportionment provisions of the Pennsylvania Constitution in 1967-68, they deliberately conceived of the existing plan as the best of both worlds. There was considerable concern about leaving the process entirely in the hands of the legislature; that approach had led to mischief and gridlock in the early part of the twentieth century and was the precise reason that the 1967-68 Constitutional Convention was directed to target reapportionment for change.[393] At the same time, the framers had balked at entirely taking reapportionment out of the hands of the political leaders and placing the responsibility in the hands of "neutral" parties such as judges.[394] The political leaders possessed a wealth of experience and sensitivity to life from Bucks County to Carbon County to Westmoreland County to Center City Philadelphia. These legislators had been elected directly by the people and were in the best position to guide the process and to fashion new districts each decade. The Constitutional Convention thus settled on a middle ground, in essence, between the pure "Iowa model" and the pure "political model" in which legislators controlled the process unchecked. Under the current Article II, Section 17, the neutral Chairman was injected into the equation to moderate political interests and act as a swing vote.

The question of shifting to an Iowa model is in any event an academic one, since any change in the Commonwealth's reapportionment process would require a constitutional amendment. Furthermore, the Commission's experience in 1991 confirmed that the presence of political leaders and their staffs in the reapportionment process is virtually indispensable in such a fast-paced mission, particularly if districts are to be created that reflect the natural interests, politics, and alliances of thousands of neighborhoods and communities across the Commonwealth.

B. Need for an Independent Chairman

To protect the Legislature from citizen perceptions that the legislature is unduly focussed on preserving incumbencies, and to carry out the constitutional scheme envisioned by Article II, Section 17, it is absolutely essential that the Chairman play an active, independent role in future reapportionments. The independent Chairman, in the minds of the constitutional draftsmen, distinguished the current Pennsylvania system from the previous (unsatisfactory) approach controlled entirely by the legislature.

A number of steps might be taken to achieve fine-tuning on this front. First, the Chairman should be selected early, perhaps six months in advance of the actual reapportionment. He or she should have an opportunity to begin to absorb the mass of material involving population data, legal precedent, past reapportionment history, and other information before stepping into office. Likewise, the supporting framework for the Chairman should be prepared by the ultimate Commission members (i.e. the Majority and Minority Leaders of the House and Senate) at least one year in advance of the formal start of the reapportionment process. No need exists to wait for the federal census before building the structure into which the Chairman will be placed. Details such as locating office space, assembling desks

---

[393] *See supra* Section II.C.
[394] *Id.*

and equipment, and ordering supplies all constitute tasks that can be accomplished well in advance. These mundane chores detract considerably from the work of the Chairman and his staff members in the fast-moving, 90-day reapportionment whirlwind.

In preparing for the Chairman and other Commission members, the Legislative Data Processing Center should play an increasingly pivotal role. As the nonpartisan office in the Capitol that shoulders the heaviest responsibility in reapportionment, LDPC should be given the allocations and mandates necessary to begin its work long before the actual Commission is assembled. Indeed, LDPC possesses sufficient expertise and computer technology to maintain and update boundary descriptions throughout the Commonwealth on an ongoing basis so that this work can be completed long before reapportionment begins. Although keeping such data current is to a certain extent dependent upon a diligent response by the Bureau of Elections, LDPC is in the best position to prod that agency. LDPC is also in a position to train staff and build upon the expertise of past reapportionment efforts so that a highly sophisticated team of employees is in place before the start of each decade.

Most critical to the independent operation of the Commission Chairman in future reapportionments will be the establishment, before the Chairman is selected, of a central computer operation. This should be available to the Chairman and each Commission member's staff from the inception of the reapportionment process. During the past two reapportionments, to ensure intra-party confidentiality, each political caucus (via each political Commission member) funded and purchased its own computer equipment for tabulating data and sketching maps. Although there is nothing wrong with each caucus creating its own facility if it wishes, it is absolutely essential that the Chairman have access to a central independent computer system dedicated primarily to the use of the Commission. The ability to generate maps and interpret population data is tantamount to the ability to hold a pen and employ a cartographer under the old-fashioned method of mapmaking. The Chairman will never achieve true independence, or make fully informed decisions, without the ability to produce his or her own maps and to analyze his or her own data free from the partisan nudges that necessarily guide the caucuses. Moreover, a uniform set of maps and data would greatly facilitate negotiations among the Commission members and the Chairman. Rather than circulating four different printouts, databases, and sets of numbers, all Commission members would be operating from the same documents. Common maps and data would also prove beneficial in allowing the Secretary of the Commonwealth to publish maps of the Preliminary and Final Plans for citizen review, in a prompt fashion, as mandated by Article II, Section 17.

Once in place, a central computer system could be staffed by nonpartisan personnel, perhaps through LDPC, and become immediately accessible to the Chairman and each Commission member as the Commission begins its work. The Chairman would then be in a position to hire his or her own advisor and/or technician, if desired, to ensure full independence.

Finally, the creation of a strong, autonomous Chairman and staff would yield other benefits as the reapportionment process unfolds. Once reapportionment moves into its inevitable litigation phase, certain Commission members are unavoidably in the position of "adversaries" with respect to the Commission *qua* body. At some point, the Chairman and his or her staff are the only nonpolitical actors in a position to guide litigation strategy via counsel, make independent decisions concerning expenditures, and otherwise keep the Commission afloat in a way that protects the Commission as a body. This was the case, for instance, in the Chester County litigation in 1993, which squarely pitted Democratic and Republican interests in the battle over the relocation of Senator Pecora's seat in eastern Pennsylvania.[395] To the extent that the Chairman can be viewed as apolitical, this will go a long way to instill confidence in citizens and politicians alike.

C. Enhanced Opportunity for Citizen Participation

Throughout the reapportionment process, the Commission was faced with a stream of requests from citizens and groups seeking data and maps useful in generating their own proposals. The Commission took a consistent stand in favor of liberal public access to official data and maps.[396] At the same time, early in the reapportionment process, some groups like the NAACP criticized the Commission for not providing racial data in a prompt and usable fashion.[397] The Puerto Rican Legal Defense and Education Fund chastised the Commission for not providing computer terminals and software that would allow citizens to sit in an office and create their own proposed reapportionment plans, as was done in New York City.[398]

The Commission did go to great lengths to provide population data and racial data to all those making requests. The data was provided on a computer disc, as well as in hard copy, free of charge. However, it became clear that with the advent of the computer age in reapportionment, more will have to be done in future reapportionments to ensure meaningful public participation.

The key will be to distinguish between official data used by the Commission to generate a plan, which should be made immediately accessible to the public, and the actual *work product* of the Commission members and their staffs, which must remain privileged. Census data, revisions to the census data made by LDPC, racial data, voting age population, past voting statistics, political affiliation data, the Preliminary Plan, and the Final Plan should all be made available to the public at minimal cost. These constitute official data and serve as the raw materials with which the Commission itself generates its Preliminary and Final Plans. The same raw materials should be available to allow a citizen or group to generate his or her own maps and proposals. On the other hand, working maps generated by the Commission members and their staffs proposing districts for purposes of negotiating and the notes of Commission members and their staffs should be off limits. These are unofficial documents that constitute the work product of the Commission as it seeks to forge a statewide plan in just ninety days.

Just as the legislature and its members are not forced to divulge the considerable documents that go into strategizing and negotiating over a piece of legislation before it is formally proposed, it would result in chaos if every step of the Commission's work were exposed to public scrutiny. All meetings of the Chairman and Commission members (i.e. where a quorum is present) must be held in public; only here can official business be conducted. However, much of the Commission's preliminary work is accomplished by staff members and individual Commission

[395] *See supra* Section XII.

[396] *See supra* text accompanying notes 156-57.

[397] *See supra* text accompanying notes 200-01.

[398] Letter from Arthur A. Baer, Associate Counsel, Puerto Rican Legal Defense and Education Fund to Ken Gormley, Executive Director, Pennsylvania Legislative Reapportionment Commission (Aug. 21, 1991) (State Archives).

members meeting informally with the Chairman to negotiate tentative districts and compromises. To force the Commission to make public this confidential work product, or to hold all such negotiations in public, would essentially grind the process to a halt. Individual legislators, whose jobs are at stake, would know the every move of the Commission and make coexistence in the Capitol impossible. Citizen lobbies and concerned groups would be on hand to debate every square inch of the 45,000-square mile Pennsylvania map, making productive negotiation within the Commission unattainable.

The key to a fair, workable definition of public access is to delineate between official data and unofficial work product of the Commission; the latter must remain private for the Commission just as it remains private for the legislature and indeed for citizens themselves engaging in the reapportionment exercise. This was the general approach taken by the 1991 Commission, just as it was taken by the 1981 Commission.[399] The ground rules in this respect should be established firmly, in writing, and made available to the public early on to avoid confusion.

The other key to ensuring true public participation in the reapportionment process is to guarantee that all actual decision-making takes place at duly advertised public meetings. Debate should be open, candid, and on the record so that citizens understand the forces motivating each Commission member and have a basis for appealing to the Pennsylvania Supreme Court if dissatisfied with the Preliminary or Final Plan. Although it is a natural instinct of those potentially involved in litigation, and their counsel, to remain tight-lipped in order to avoid providing ammunition to opponents, the Commission possesses a special obligation to avoid such a stonewall approach. Like the legislature, the Commission has a duty to vigorously debate the issues, cast votes in public, and allow citizens a realistic chance to participate in the process. Only in this fashion can enhanced public access to data, and greater sophistication in technology, prove meaningful to the average citizen. Unfortunately, the 1971 and 1981 Commissions left behind a scant public record and provided slim documentation to the courts as the reapportionment appeals were considered. The Commission of 1991 sought to reverse this trend. Future Commissions should work harder to build a full, meaningful record at public meetings and hearings that can ultimately guide review of the Final Plan in the Pennsylvania Supreme Court.

D. More Meaningful Pennsylvania Supreme Court Review

It has become evident after three decades' worth of Pennsylvania Supreme Court review of reapportionment plans that the Court itself is saddled with several difficult and somewhat anomalous functions never clearly thought out by the framers of Article II, Section 17. First, reapportionment is sprung on the Court, much like it is sprung on the legislature, in ten year intervals and with little forewarning. The Court, unlike the legislature, receives no official notice that the gears of reapportionment have begun grinding until it is presented with a *fait accompli*. After a Final Plan is filed, dozens of petitions objecting to the Final Plan pour into the Prothonotary's Office of the Pennsylvania Supreme Court. It is not until this late hour that the seven Justices and their staffs are made formally aware of this massive project that must be completed in short order. Because the membership of

---

[399] *See* Minutes, 8th meeting 1981.

the Court turns over considerably every ten years, there are typically only several Justices who have gone through a reapportionment in the previous decade.[400] All of this means that the entire process comes as a staggering and novel surprise to most members of the Court and their staffs.

The Commission can aid the Court, in future years, by keeping the Court apprised of its timetables well in advance. Counsel for the Commission should write informally to the Chief Justice at the outset of the reapportionment process, informing him or her of the constitutional deadlines for the Preliminary and Final Plans as determined by the Commission. Counsel might also inform the Court of any novel legal issues that are likely to arise during the course of reapportionment,[401] so long as this is done in a non-partisan fashion and with the blessing of the political members of the Commission. Such courtesy status reports by the Commission's Counsel might give the seven Justices an opportunity to familiarize themselves with a decade's worth of reapportionment law and allow their clerks to begin assembling research materials and case law in an orderly fashion. It would also allow for advance planning regarding a suitable date to hear the dozens of reapportionment appeals, rather than last-minute phone calls announcing a hurried date with only several days' notice. The latter only diminishes the efficacy of briefs and oral arguments for all concerned.

Second, the Pennsylvania Supreme Court faces a quandary when it sits *en banc* to hear the deluge of reapportionment petitions. The Supreme Court is by nature an appellate body. It almost exclusively reviews decisions of lower state courts and renders opinions as to their legal sufficiency. The Court is neither equipped to act, nor experienced to act, as an initial fact-finding body. The problem is that the draftsmen of Article II, Section 17 never thought through this significant detail. A sea of petitions pours into the Court, each raising factual allegations and assertions concerning statements and actions of Commission members, legislators, and petitioners; such "facts," however, have never been determined by a lower court or jury. The Court is thus left to act as an appellate court reviewing a factual record that is virtually nonexistent, other than transcripts of the Commission's meetings and its official documents, thereby placing the Court in an awkward hybrid position.

Clearly, the intention of the draftsmen of Article II, Section 17 was to allow a speedy review of the Final Plan to avoid the disruption of primary and general elections. On the large run of issues, the Court is able to observe the Plan on its face and determine whether it is consistent with the laws of Pennsylvania, giving deference as a rule to the Commission, just as it does to the legislature. However, it is at least possible to envision issues on which the Court might wish to clarify factual matters before rendering a final decision. For instance, in the 1991 Reapportionment the Court was clearly troubled during oral argument by last minute changes made to the Final Plan that effectively drew Clifford Jones and Larry

---

[400] In 1991, only Chief Justice Nix and Justice Flaherty had previous reapportionment experience. Justice Larsen, while on the Supreme Court in 1981, did not participate in the 1991 reapportionment appeals. *In re* 1991 Pennsylvania Reapportionment Comm'n, 530 Pa. 335, 609 A.2d 132 (1992), *cert. denied sub nom.* Loeper v. Pennsylvania Legislative Reapportionment Comm'n, 113 S. Ct. 66 (1992).

[401] For instance, the Federal Voting Rights Act was known to be a central issue in the 1991 Reapportionment. It is uncertain, however, whether the Court had any reason to appreciate the magnitude of this issue, which had never figured into previous state reapportionments, until it sat down, read the briefs, and listened to oral argument.

Roberts out of districts in which they had publicly announced their intentions to run.[402] Although the Court ultimately found that these changes did not rise to the level of "political gerrymandering" or deny petitioners a "right to run for a particular office," the allegations were clearly unsettling to the Court.[403] Certain Justices were particularly troubled by the fact that such changes were made *after* the Preliminary Plan was filed and advertised, stripping petitioners of any realistic opportunity to lodge challenges with the Commission. The Court, however, lacked any mechanism to develop the facts on this issue, since the "record" from the Commission was utterly silent on this score.

Similarly, several aspects of Federal Voting Rights Act challenges were awkward for the Court. The Commission had retained an expert on voting rights matters, Dr. Richard Engstrom, who had guided the Commission throughout its work and advised the Commission that its plan was consistent with federal law. Dr. Engstrom, however, never testified before the Commission. His opinions were nowhere "of record" except as summarized by Chairman Cindrich at public hearings. The Court was thus justifiably puzzled as to how to deal with Engstrom's conclusions. The Commission submitted an affidavit of Engstrom to the Court, which was discussed in briefs and oral argument. However, the affidavit was never referred to in the Court's final opinion because it did not officially contain "facts" of record. Likewise, many factual assertions raised by the Voting Rights Act petitioners concerning the viability of 60% minority Senate districts in Philadelphia revolved around a loose array of allegations and "facts" never established definitively in any court.

In instances such as these, the Pennsylvania Supreme Court should be afforded a mechanism to develop "facts" to its satisfaction, if it desires to delve deeper. Certainly, it would be only in extraordinary circumstances perhaps not present in the 1991 Reapportionment that the Court would wish to move beyond the map and official Commission record to determine if a Final Plan was lawful. However, in the rare case where factors such as the motives of the Commission or blurred factual data come into play, the Court should have the ability to build a factual record sufficient to discharge its constitutional function of review.

The immediate solution, given the obvious gap in Article II, Section 17 on this score, is for the Court itself to take the initiative to hold a special fact-finding hearing — or direct a lower court or special master to do so — if an extraordinary issue of fact presents itself. In the long run, the proper solution will be for the legislature and voters to amend Article II, Section 17, to iron out such thirty-year-old bugs.

E. Minority Voting Rights — Preparing for the Future

Just as the final appeals were being put to rest in connection with the Reapportionment of 1991, the United States Supreme Court was changing the face of Federal Voting Rights Act precedent once again. In *Shaw v. Reno*,[404] decided in the summer of 1993, the Court issued a dramatic ruling involving North Carolina's congressional reapportionment. Here, a divided Court held that a 160-mile-long

---

[402] *See supra* Section X.C.

[403] *See In re* 1991 Pennsylvania Legislative Reapportionment Comm'n, 530 Pa. 335, 355-56, 609 A.2d 132, 141-42 (1992), *cert. denied sub nom.* Loeper v. Pennsylvania Legislative Reapportionment Comm'n, 113 S. Ct. 66 (1992).

[404] 113 S. Ct. 2816 (1993).

district that snaked its way along Interstate 85 to create a majority African-American enclave constituted a potential violation of the Equal Protection Clause and in effect amounted to reverse racial gerrymandering. Justice Sandra Day O'Connor authored the majority opinion, holding that the unsightly, contorted majority African-American district "resembles the most egregious racial gerrymanders of the past."[405] Although acknowledging that "race-conscious redistricting is not always unconstitutional,"[406] Justice O'Connor wrote in stern language that "[a] reapportionment plan that includes in one district individuals ... who may have little in common with one another but the color of their skin, bears an uncomfortable relationship to political apartheid."[407]

The proper approach for the Court in analyzing such blatant racial gerrymandering, wrote Justice O'Connor, was to apply the "strict scrutiny" standard. Only if a reapportionment plan is "narrowly tailored to further a compelling governmental interest" will it be upheld under the Equal Protection Clause.[408] Justice O'Connor made clear that the Court was expressing no opinion as to whether "the intentional creation of majority-minority districts, without more" *always* gave rise to an equal protection claim.[409] However, when the district is so dramatically irregular and departs from the traditional guideposts of compactness, contiguity, and respect for political boundaries that it cannot be understood as anything other than an effort to "segregate voters" on the basis of race, the strict scrutiny standard of the Equal Protection Clause must apply.[410]

It is far from clear whether the Supreme Court's decision in *Shaw* signals a rethinking of the *Thornburg v. Gingles* standard which so powerfully drove the Pennsylvania Reapportionment of 1991. Although some newspaper accounts viewed *Shaw* as a major overhaul in redistricting jurisprudence,[411] the undercurrent of Justice O'Connor's opinion in *Shaw* seems to be that race-based districts are still permissible, and indeed mandated, by the Voting Rights Act *up to a point.*[412] At some point, however, the creation of race-based districts becomes so contorted and unlike the norm that strict scrutiny must be employed. In such instances, only if the majority-minority district is "narrowly tailored to further a compelling governmental interest" can such a blatant creation be upheld under the Equal Protection Clause.

If *Shaw* suggests anything, clearly it is that federal law surrounding the Voting Rights Act has a long way to grow. In the next decade, *Gingles* and its progeny will undoubtedly need further refinement as the courts walk the delicate balance between prohibiting "political apartheid" and allowing African-Americans and minorities a fighting chance in an electoral system that was for centuries stacked against them.

---

[405] 113 S. Ct. at 2824.

[406] *Id.*

[407] *Id.* at 2817.

[408] *Id.* at 2825.

[409] *Id.* at 2828.

[410] *Id.* at 2826-2827.

[411] *See, e.g.,* Dick Lehr, *Court casts doubts over race-based redistricting,* THE BOSTON GLOBE, June 29, 1993.

[412] Indeed, Justice O'Connor authored a concurrence in *Gingles* which indicated a willingness to go even *further* than the majority in creating majority-minority and minority-influenced districts. *See* Thornburg v. Gingles, 478 U.S. 30, 83 (1986) (O'Connor, J., concurring).

Regardless of the evolution of federal law in this area, the Pennsylvania Legislative Reapportionment Commission must remain sensitive to the evolving needs of minority-citizens as a matter of history and equality. Pennsylvania voluntarily created districts capable of electing minority representatives in the House and the Senate long before the Federal Voting Rights Act issued a national mandate on this score. The key to a healthy electoral system in the Commonwealth, for future generations, will depend upon the Commission's willingness to continue to tinker and to take firm stands to protect the right of African-Americans, Latinos, and other minority groups to elect candidates of choice, regardless of the changing winds of federal precedent.[413]

---

[413] Article I, Section 26 of the Pennsylvania Constitution may indeed compel this.

XIV.
CONCLUSION

The lessons from the Pennsylvania Reapportionment of 1991 are plentiful and positive for future Commissions, legislators, citizens, and scholars alike. In its third incarnation, the Commission faced a downpour of new issues and controversies, some politically explosive, others legally intricate. Yet the Commission rose to all challenges, adapting itself as a body and producing a Final Plan that withstood more attacks in the courts than any previous reapportionment plan in the Commonwealth's history.

With new issues blossoming under the Federal Voting Rights Act and populations in Pennsylvania continuing to shift, the reapportionment ritual has become much more pressing and personal for individual citizens. If the experience of 1991 proved anything, it is that the age of citizen participation is upon us.

So, too, is an era of dependence upon an active, independent Chairman. The proliferation of new technology necessarily entails a harnessing of human advancements for the benefit of greater debate and citizen participation, rather than falling backwards into the secretive shadows that dominated reapportionment in the first half of the 20th century.

That, after all, was the precise vision of the framers of Article II, Section 17, when they assembled in Harrisburg in 1967 and 1968 to amend the Pennsylvania Constitution. The result was intended to be a system, unique to Pennsylvania, that allowed a healthy dose of political input and recognized the absolute value of political expertise reposing in the legislature, while at the same time ensuring that the interests of the citizens would ultimately guide the swing vote.

The genius of the Pennsylvania system is that it blends old-fashioned political bartering and grass-roots wisdom with a healthy dose of neutral dispassion, vested in the Chairman. As long as this delicate balance is preserved, in the spirit of the Constitution itself, each future Commission will continue to experiment and grow in the face of challenges that no living human being, in any previous generation, could have ever forseen. Such is the beauty, indeed the essence, of the American democratic experiment.

APPENDIX A
CONSTITUTION OF THE
COMMONWEALTH OF PENNSYLVANIA
ARTICLE II — THE LEGISLATURE

Legislative Districts

Section 16. The Commonwealth shall be divided into 50 senatorial and 203 representative districts, which shall be composed of compact and contiguous territory as nearly equal in population as practicable. Each senatorial district shall elect one Senator, and each representative district one Representative. Unless absolutely necessary no county, city, incorporated town, borough, township or ward shall be divided in forming either a senatorial or representative district.

Legislative Reapportionment Commission

Section 17. (a) In each year following the year of the Federal decennial census, a Legislative Reapportionment Commission shall be constituted for the purpose of reapportioning the Commonwealth. The commission shall act by a majority of its entire membership.

(b) The commission shall consist of five members: four of whom shall be the majority and minority leaders of both the Senate and the House of Representatives, or deputies appointed by each of them, and a chairman selected as hereinafter provided. No later than 60 days following the official reporting of the Federal decennial census as required by Federal law, the four members shall be certified by the President pro tempore of the Senate and the Speaker of the House of Representatives to the elections officer of the Commonwealth who under law shall have supervision over elections.

The four members within 45 days after their certification shall select the fifth member, who shall serve as chairman of the commission, and shall immediately certify his name to such elections officer. The chairman shall be a citizen of the Commonwealth other than a local, State or Federal official holding an office to which compensation is attached.

If the four members fail to select the fifth member within the time prescribed, a majority of the entire membership of the Supreme Court within 30 days thereafter shall appoint the chairman as aforesaid and certify his appointment to such elections officer.

Any vacancy in the commission shall be filled within 15 days in the same manner in which such position was originally filled.

(c) No later than 90 days after either the commission has been duly certified or the population data for the Commonwealth as determined by the Federal decennial census are available, whichever is later in time, the commission shall file a preliminary reapportionment plan with such elections officer.

The commission shall have 30 days after filing the preliminary plan to make corrections in the plan.

Any person aggrieved by the preliminary plan shall have the same 30-day period to file exceptions with the commission in which case the commission shall have 30 days after the date the exceptions were filed to prepare and file with such elections officer a revised reapportionment plan. If no exceptions are filed within 30 days, or if filed and acted upon, the commission's plan shall be final and have the force of law.

(d) Any aggrieved person may file an appeal from the final plan directly to the Supreme Court within 30 days after the filing thereof. If the appellant establishes that the final plan is contrary to law, the Supreme Court shall issue an order remanding the plan to the commission and directing the commission to reapportion the Commonwealth in a manner not inconsistent with such order.

(e) When the Supreme Court has finally decided an appeal or when the last day for filing an appeal has passed with no appeal taken, the reapportionment plan shall have the force of law and the districts therein provided shall be used thereafter in elections to the General Assembly until the next reapportionment as required under this section 17.

(f) The General Assembly shall appropriate sufficient funds for the compensation and expenses of members and staff appointed by the commission, and other necessary expenses. The members of the commission shall be entitled to such compensation for their services as the General Assembly from time to time shall determine, but no part thereof shall be paid until a preliminary plan is filed. If a preliminary plan is filed but the commission fails to file a revised or final plan within the time prescribed, the commission members shall forfeit all right to compensation not paid.

(g) If a preliminary, revised or final reapportionment plan is not filed by the commission within the time prescribed by this section, unless the time be extended by the Supreme Court for cause shown, the Supreme Court shall immediately proceed on its own motion to reapportion the Commonwealth.

(h) Any reapportionment plan filed by the commission, or ordered or prepared by the Supreme Court upon the failure of the commission to act, shall be published by the elections officer once in at least one newspaper of general circulation in each senatorial and representative district. The publication shall contain a map of the Commonwealth showing the complete reapportionment of the General Assembly by districts, and a map showing the reapportioned districts in the area normally served by the newspaper in which the publication is made. The publication shall also state the population of the senatorial and representative districts having the smallest and largest population and the percentage variation of such districts from the average population for senatorial and representative districts.

TABLE OF CASES

INDEX